FATHER, SON,

AND

SOLDERING GUN

FATHER, SON,

AND

SOLDERING GUN

Stories
That
Forge Us

STEVEN V. MYCYNEK

Published by Dackel Books, Somerville, Massachusetts. For more information, please contact info@dackelbooks.com | https://www.dackelbooks.com

I assert that all stories and dialogue are true and factual to the best of my recollection.

All quotations referenced have been researched as accurate and correctly attributed to the best of my ability.

Lyrics from KMFDM's "Trust" used with permission from Sasha Konietzko and Metropolis records.

Cover design by Amanda Bartlett
Typesetting by Colleen Jones

ISBN 979-8-9893885-0-9 Paperback
ISBN 979-8-9893885-1-6 eBook

Library of Congress Control Number: 2023924708

CONTENTS

CONTENTS

Do what you can
What you want
What you must
Feel the hunger inside
Hold on to your trust

—"Trust" by KMFDM

DEDICATION

To Ashna, Garrison, Elliot, and anyone else who looked at what their dad got them for Christmas and wondered "What the heck is this?" To Jim Marsh, who ultimately inspired this book by asking why I was making a 3D solid model of a paper business card I saw in a movie twenty years ago.

ACKNOWLEDGMENTS

Thank you to my editors, Pamela Sourelis and Dori Harrell, as well as all my friends at PTC/Onshape who encouraged me to keep writing, and of course, my wife, Rima, who always supports me despite the messy, overgrown workshop I call my personality. Thank you also to Sasha Konietzko, KMFDM, and Metropolis records for permission to use a song lyric excerpt.

INTRODUCTION

E veryone's different in their own way. Arguably, that's a bit of an empty statement, but I challenge you to consider it for a moment. I will gamble it is worth your time as you keep reading.

I'm certainly not the smartest, weirdest, edgiest, cleverest, geekiest, or any other superlative you can think of, but I've never met anyone who didn't conclude that I was a little odd. Whether they considered that a positive or a negative is the only thing that's changed over the years. As I grew older, I looked at all the lumps and grooves in my personality and admitted that they'll never be sanded down.

This admission surfaced when recently, over a drink, I showed a friend how, in my free time, I modeled the shape of a business card in three dimensions and made the actual printed ink a three-dimensional solid body with mass and modeled the indentation in the cardstock where the ink sat.

My friend worked near but still a bit outside the rather narrow industry I work in, so he had to ask "Why?" All I could come up with was "I just can't help myself. I have to."[1] We laughed, and I admitted I had my quirks and in middle age was just now realizing how pronounced they were. I knew the real explanation, but I couldn't put it into words until a day or two later. To give the real answer, I needed to write down a story. One story turned into two. I ended up writing an entire book just to answer my friend's *why*. I invite you to look back on your own life as you read this—maybe you'll end up writing a book of your own.

So . . . why? My dad was born in 1943 and died in 2004. He was an electrical engineer at Zenith Electronics in Glenview, Illinois, who'd designed digital and analog circuits for television systems for nearly forty years. He was also a self-taught extreme handyman and jack-of-all-trades—once described as "an engineer's engineer." I don't know a lot about his earlier years, since he grew up poor, without much family, but as you'll see, I've pieced together a bit.

---

1 The technical reason is that I wanted to isolate the printing geometry from the paper geometry so I could later adjust its texture or shape more effectively in ways beyond font or line spacing. Plus, I was doing some font-related work at my job, so this project explored that a bit.

Introduction

I was born in 1977, so I grew up in the eighties and nineties and have plenty of memories from that time. My dad was a lot like me, with a lot of pronounced peaks, valleys, rough edges, and other unexpected contours in his personality. When I got married, my mom was worried that my messy, disorganized personality might be too much for my wife, so she took her aside at the reception and said, "He's a good man, and he's a lot like his father. Just don't ever look in any of his desk drawers and you'll be happy."

It's become clear, sometimes painfully, sometimes hilariously, that I'm my father's son, and the only way I can explain it all is through stories. The events from these stories made me. They forged me. I claim that your stories also forged you, and accepting your stories, never hiding from them, will unlock your potential more than any other choice you make in life.

NOTEBOOK PAPER

The true hero is always a hero by mistake; he dreams of being an honest coward like everybody else.

—Romain Rolland

1991

My dad had a reputation for doing things for people, even if they weren't typical, obvious, or well understood.

He was a man of action. If he was sitting, which wasn't often, he was likely reading *Scientific American* or *Science News*, but mostly he was doing something, somewhere, all hours of the day. He did watch television, but even that was a special activity, as I'll explain in a later story.

One morning when I was twelve, I was eating breakfast and getting ready for school. My mom had the radio on, listening to the Roy Leonard morning show, and my dad was looking at *Science News* as usual. Our house was a three-bedroom ranch in the northwest suburbs of Chicago, and like many families of that era, we spent most of our time together around the kitchen table.

I packed up my backpack at breakfast while taking short breaks from Cheerios and milk. I was a messy, disorganized child, and this was a messy, disorganized daily chore, probably better done the night before, especially since I grew up in the peak bulky school-supply years—in the era of Trapper Keepers but before email. After I gave all my books and homework a final once-over, heard my mom complain about how I always waited "till the last minute," and stuffed a few last papers into the folders they hopefully belonged, I looked at my binder and remarked, "Oh, I'm out of notebook paper."

Despite the tornado-ravaged pawn shop that was my mind, I was a good student, so this was more of an "oops, things happen" moment. Anyway, I figured I'd be fine sweeping this under the rug and went back to eating and daydreaming about what would be on TV in the afternoon. Like many children, I liked school—I just didn't like the routine of going to school, so of course I gravitated toward anything that could be a distraction at 7:30 in the morning.

After about ten minutes of finishing up but before heading off to the bus stop, as I did my usual "Bye, Mom!" I took a quick look around and asked, "Where's Dad?" I had not noticed that he'd disappeared.

I wandered down the hall and found that he had gone to the computer and started up AutoSketch (a consumer version of AutoCAD, a tool used in architectural and mechanical design). The old DOS version of AutoSketch seems horribly primitive by today's standards, but it was an enormously effective tool for creating precision line drawings.

In AutoSketch, my dad had drawn out some wide-ruled notebook lines, added a margin marker, printed out twenty copies, and put them through our three-hole punch, ready for my three-ring binder. Instant spare looseleaf notebook paper! A simple "Here, I made this" was all I got from him. My reaction then was simultaneously stunned but also somehow not-at-all-surprised—sort of like now, when my wife runs a thirteen-mile obstacle course through mud, inverted walls, and barbed wire.

This is just one of countless times when my dad would slip away to take care of something. He never talked about it. I always found out secondhand about something he did. I'd be at home on the weekend in grade school, high school, or college, and I'd ask, "Where's Dad?" and my mom would tell me he was tutoring junior high kids. Or he'd be giving people from church who were too old to drive a ride to the grocery store. "He's putting up shelves for someone." "He goes over and picks up trash by the school on Saturdays." Or he was out shoveling snow for older neighbors—that one I'd help him with sometimes. But in general, my dad just popped up all over the place, took care of things, and then would be on his way to do something else before anyone noticed, like a low-key Batman of suburban tasks.

I had some inkling my dad was a little different in this sense, but it was a vague feeling. I was a kid—the gravity of how people spend their time was still a little lost on me back then.

Fast-forward thirteen years to when I lived in Boston for my new job after college.

One Monday my mom left a voicemail on my work phone and cell within two minutes. Dad's heart had stopped beating that morning. I flew back home to Chicago.

There were more people at my dad's funeral than there would be at my wedding years later. Keep in mind, my father was not a politician, a celebrity, a CEO, or a business owner. He wasn't an artist or

in the military. He didn't live through the era of social media influencers. Still, we had to tell people to
come in shifts just to make time to meet everyone.

My mom was a school nurse, and the staff from
all four schools she worked at came by. We picked up
a party plate of Subway sandwiches for the family to
eat at the visitation—I burned enough calories greeting people and telling stories about Dad that I had
to sit down and eat something once in a while just
to keep on going. Just masses and masses of people;
I was meeting many of them for the first time. My
dad's barber was there! Never in my entire life had
I met so many people in one day, people who had
all experienced something like my dad printing up
a batch of notebook paper for them at a moment's
notice.[2]

The reach my dad's existence had is a lot to live
up to. In my sadder moments, I feel like I'll never
come close to doing what he did. I have all sorts of
reasons—I've moved a lot, I work too much, I don't
understand people. However, maybe none of us is
equipped to fully know how much our actions matter in the moment. Could my dad have known the
size of the crowd that would be at his funeral? He

---

2 I almost forgot—I've spent nearly my entire career in CAD—at
Revit, Dassault/SolidWorks, Autodesk, and PTC/Onshape. I wonder
how that happened.

was probably too busy to ever ponder such a thing. Should I change my life to make more of a difference? Is it even possible? I don't think my dad tried to do this. He was just being—the only way he knew how.

PINEWOOD DERBY

Somebody put in the wrench time.
—Johnny Tran, *The Fast and the Furious*

1987

I was a Cub Scout from about second to fourth grade. Scouts had many activities, most of which I could have taken or left, but one I absolutely loved was the annual Pinewood Derby—a tournament where a Scout and his father would build a small wooden race car the size of a chalkboard eraser from a kit (basically, a wooden block and four plastic wheels). The Scouts would then host a double-elimination tournament, racing them down a ramp, with a few hundred kids participating. It was great fun and probably the only thing I ever competed in as a child.

My dad wasn't a carpenter, but he had a large selection of tools in the basement, which he worked with whenever he could—we called it his workshop—so when I was nine, we were excited to build that car together.

"Dad, what do we have to do after we put the wheels on?" I asked.

"It's a little more than just that—you'll see," Dad replied.

Unless I wanted my race car to look like a semitruck trailer, I'd have to carve away a lot of wood. We drew some lines on the block and sawed off the first major corners with a hacksaw. We sanded, sawed again, sanded again, gradually cutting away corners upon corners, and after a few days finally made some progress producing a shape that looked like either a simple race car, or at least a decent Dustbuster.

"Now we paint it?" I asked.

"If we paint it now, the wood will be rough and uneven. We need to seal the wood first before priming and painting."

We rubbed sanding sealer, a noxious varnish-like goop, on to the wooden body with an old undershirt—quickly—and then ran upstairs to get away from the fumes. After a half hour, we came back down, sanded the wood, applied more goop, ran upstairs, and repeated the process two more times.

I sanded with finer and finer paper until my hands hurt, but when we were done, the wood surface felt like glass.

The tournament specified a weight limit for the cars, and we were encouraged to use lead fishing weights to get the car as close to the limit as possible. Even with weights, my car was thirty or forty grams under the limit.

"Let's use the wide-boring drill bits—we can drill some holes in the back of the car and put pennies in the back, adding them one by one until we're at the right weight," Dad said.

After loading the car up with enough spare change to be just under the limit, I sealed them in place with my sister's nail polish. You can still see Lincoln's face covered in sparkly purple where the license plate would go.

I suppose we could have put the wheels on and been done, but apparently we weren't. My dad told me we needed to grind the wheel axles with steel wool. We put each axle from the kit (they were nails—very high tech) into a power drill, and we polished them with a few grades of steel wool until each one shone like silver. I didn't totally get it at the time—the nails seemed fine out of the box, and they were going on the bottom of the car anyway—but I followed along.

The next thing we built was an "alignment box."

Again, I wasn't really following this, but my dad got out his T-square, some two-by-fours, and some wood screws, and we built a frame a little larger than the car.

"Before you race the car, press the car in each direction in the box to square up the wheels," my dad said.

I didn't really understand—the car rolled, the wheels turned—but we did this, again and again, each time we rolled the car, and my dad told me that keeping the car in good condition, aligned, clean, and dust-free was key. I swore "alignment" was his favorite word that week. We kept the car in a padded shoebox after we were finished the final tweaks.

There was one other relevant detail of the Pinewood Derby I learned as the tournament grew closer. This was back in the eighties, when divorce became much more common and talked about. But people were still getting over the stigma and figuring out how to deal with it socially, so the Cub Scouts group in my area had a program where one of the dads who had a professional machine shop would gather all the kids who didn't have a father around and help them build their cars.

There was a kid from my grade school who was one of those boys—Cal. I never liked him—he was this smug, aloof kid with this "Don't Mess with Texas" T-shirt he wore all the time—but anyway, he didn't have a dad, so he got one of the machine-shop cars.

Cal brought his car to school a few days before the race, and it was a spectacle that drew the other kids into a small crowd. It looked professionally made. It was stunning—a perfectly smooth hood, deep-purple paint, and a wide white racing stripe down the middle. It was so glossy you could see your face in it. Wow!

On the day of the Pinewood Derby, guess who I had to race first?

Cal.

I was so angry and jealous. I resented him and the fancy car he didn't even build. Hey, I was nine—what could you expect? I thought for certain I would lose, and it wasn't fair. But rules were rules, and the Cub Scout officials placed both cars up at the top of the ramp, released the lever, and my car sped down the track.

Cal's car didn't move at all from the starting line.

While he had this band-saw-carved aerodynamic hood profile and high-end paint job with racing stripes, the axles holding his wheels were so crooked, the car wouldn't even roll. That stalled car on the track almost looked lifeless, like a sick animal, and instantly my resentment turned to guilt and sorrow. The surface-level guidance that machine-shop dad gave all those kids had its limits.

I think the judges might have bent things back into place for Cal, but he was still soon eliminated from the competition, and I went on to win third place out of about three hundred kids.

A year after that race, Cal and I went to different schools, and I never saw him again. Still, when I have a big win in life, I'm still sometimes haunted by that moment on the track. What if I didn't have someone in my corner? How many times in life did have I had a significant advantage over others and didn't realize it at the time? Would I be better off not knowing, or is being haunted like this part of me now?

THE WORKSHOP

Creative minds are rarely tidy.
—Carl Jung

1988

I have many other stories I could tell you about my
dad's workshop. As I said, he wasn't a carpenter
or a mechanic—he just had half a semi-finished
basement with a lot of space for benches, shelves,
bins, cabinets, and any other type of storage you
could think of.

We had a drill press that looked like it was
from the 1930s (exposed belts and pulleys, no safe-
ty guards of any kind), saws of different sizes and
shapes, hammers, files, planes, wire cutters, pliers, tin
snips, clamps, screwdrivers, wrenches, an anvil and
vise, and every grade of sandpaper and steel wool you

could imagine, along with just about every type of wire or cable. We had flashlight bulbs, light-emitting diodes, old microchips from his office, loudspeakers from old clock radios, solder, a soldering gun, and a hot-glue gun.

"Stop using up all my nine-volt batteries! Those are expensive!" was a common complaint from my dad after I'd spend an afternoon running wires across the workbench to light up bulbs and buzzers or make electromagnets that were anything but energy efficient.

There was a one-gallon can of copper sulfate crystals we could use for copperplating things. (This is highly dangerous. Don't try this alone if you are ten.) We had house paint, spray paint, varnish, sealer, paint thinner, different kinds of oil, wood glue, hot glue, epoxy, superglue, and model airplane glue. We had duct tape, packing tape, strapping tape, even this special tape that was made of paper-thin steel that magnets would stick to. You'd have to cut it with tin snips! We had a pipe bender, a machine to put caps on bottles, odd pieces of lumber, and even an old section of railroad track that weighed about fifty pounds—that was my introduction to the concept of the I-Beam.

It wasn't that the workshop was dirty or disorganized, but it was so packed full of odds and ends, so worn, and so old and full of stains and marks that you could tell that people had spent thousands of hours there. There were so many things to work with in this basement that we used the exposed ceiling rafters as shelves. I had to stand on a chair to reach into the ceiling to get the box where we kept all the sandpaper. No matter how much we vacuumed, sawdust and metal filings still found their way into every crack, pocket, and corner of the room. The smell of freshly cut wood, oil, glue, and rubber lingered most days, even years later when we sold the house.

I laugh whenever I hear about "man caves" on the internet or on some HGTV man-cave renovations show. I have nothing against a decorated area in the basement, with a pool table and a bar with neon signs and recliners—it sounds nice, but I think Tim Taylor[3] himself would be envious of our space. It wasn't fancy or professional, but you could tell that the person who stocked this room was . . . prepared, to say the least.

I think my dad just started collecting tools and supplies whenever he saw a garage sale or a bargain

---

3 I never liked the show *Home Improvement* much—I felt it sort of claimed to be preaching more healthy and progressive masculinity but still fell short and relied on a lot of gross stereotypes and putdowns to get cheap laughs—something my dad never went for, but the general allusion fits, so you get it.

and never stopped. One time in the late eighties, he learned that the consumer trash-bag industry was moving over to a thinner trash-bag plastic to save money, so one day it was "Steven, we're going to Kmart to buy trash bags," and we bought all the stock in the store. The trunk and the backseat were filled to the brim with rolls of thicker-plastic trash bags. My mom couldn't have been thrilled that day, but we had quality trash bags for all sorts of uses and projects (besides collecting trash) probably well into the twenty-first century.

One of my favorite memories from that workshop is making small electric motors with my dad. I don't know how we got into this idea, but somehow when I was nine or ten, we decided we wanted to make an electric motor out of tin cans. You need steel cans rather than aluminum or tin, but some cans, like Diet Coke or water chestnuts, were steel, so we cut out a shape from a few cans' lids—a double-sided ax-head contour the size of an Oreo cookie. We stacked three or four of those on top of each other and drilled a hole through the centers so they could spin on an axle. We then wound some insulated wire around the center of this bundle of can-lid cutouts and left the wire ends exposed. Finally, we created a small frame to hold all this in place with a two-by-four and some leftover electrical outlet wiring boxes.

The idea was that if you suspended this setup on an axle, like a nail, within a frame, like we did, and you hooked those bare wires up to a battery (ideally a cheaper C or D cell), you'd create an electromagnet that would quickly spin the core wound with wires as it became attracted to the frame around it, which would hold another strategically placed magnet. The power connection would then break as the wires moved, but you'd have transferred enough energy to spin the core around enough that it could attach to power again, this time in reverse, giving it another boost to spin back the other way and continue the cycle.

I never made it far into advanced motor or engine design, but I was overcome by the power I could see from understanding magnets and a feedback-based system. To this day I know that if I ever need to, I can design and build a machine from nearly nothing. It might be a mechanical machine, an electrical machine, or a software machine, but a machine nonetheless—they can all be built, and built at home with ordinary, cheap, or discarded things.

Ordinary, cheap, or discarded things made up much of my world growing up. I had nice things too—I wasn't poor growing up like my dad, but was

I shaped or molded by a shiny new toy that worked out of the box? Was he? Would any of us be the same if we traded childhood basements?

THE ANVIL

I have found the iron to be my greatest friend. It never freaks out on me, never runs. Friends may come and go. But two hundred pounds is always two hundred pounds.

—Henry Rollins

1988

You've probably seen anvils before—maybe mostly in cartoons. Someone is usually dropping one on someone else or falling out of a plane tied to one. The anvil from my childhood was firmly bolted in place. I don't know if my dad installed it or if it came with the house—I just know I always looked for one in other people's houses but never found one.[4]

---

4 If you ever find a child that looks like the little brother from *Honey I Shrunk the Kids* lurking around your basement, he is probably looking for an anvil, certainly not liquor or adult magazines, so no need to worry.

This anvil in my dad's workshop was the centerpiece of all the activity in that dusty, well-worn space. It was about a hundred pounds (small for an anvil), was mounted on a bench that probably weighed three times that, and had a vise grip with a crank that could crush a steel pipe. (I'll admit I used it to crack a few walnuts.) It was easily over thirty years old when I was a kid. The iron was a dark gray turned dull blue from age and use, tiny scars over every square inch.

I used that anvil for so many things that made half of those scars. If I had anything that was broken, I could keep it in the vise grip while some glue was set. If I needed to hold something steady while I drilled a hole in it or sawed part of it off? That vise grip could keep anything still. If I needed to hammer or chisel something and needed an unbreakable surface I couldn't damage, I knew that anvil would stand ready. So many things that I cut, glued, tied, bolted, nailed, sawed, pounded, cracked, bent, shaped, soldered, or sanded rested on that anvil when I was a kid building electromagnets, model rockets, motors, telegraphs, and countless other things.

Most of what my dad and I did together involved that piece of iron. My dad and I used to mix epoxy on an index card on top of that anvil. I can only imagine how much furniture we would have ruined if we didn't have this shared space to work. Whenever something was cracked or broken—a toy, a remote control, a curling iron, a folding chair, it was always "Take it to the basement," and not long after dinner, my dad would be downstairs working on it with a screwdriver, hot glue, or solder.

I used to hit caps[5] with a hammer on that anvil for hours as a child—I found that much more satisfying that shooting them from a toy gun, and my parents probably found me using a hammer to be a less disturbing and violent way to ignite gunpowder and relieve frustration. My dad had me wear his chainsaw ear-and-eye protection helmet, but that didn't stop me from exploding thousands of those caps in the basement when I was eight, nine, and ten. It was such a bizarre combination of aggression and nerdiness, but I was just happy to have the opportunity to hit something as hard as I could for as long as I wanted. I wonder why my dad let me do this so much, but I think that even he needed a break occasionally and figured this was a better babysitter and more exercise for me than just watching television, so it was a win for everyone.

Still, there were countless hours when my dad and I worked together. We spent a lot of time building model rockets in the workshop. I started building

---

5 Caps are tiny piles of gunpowder embedded in long paper rolls that go into a toy cap pistol. You can possibly still buy them, but they're more from an era on its way out.

those rockets when I was about eight and kept on until I was eighteen and knew I couldn't keep up the hobby in a dorm room.

The thing with these rockets was that the difference between a rocket going eight hundred feet and two thousand feet had a lot to do with alignment (again, his favorite word). If the fins were straight and parallel, if the launch rod guide was perfectly in line with the rocket fuselage, that rocket would go so high into the sky, you might not get it back—an ironic punishment for doing such a good job building it. A flat, steady surface for cutting or sanding, a place to put a level, a place to keep things fixed in space, this is what my dad and I talked about all the time over that anvil.

I can still see my dad standing over that anvil holding a soldering iron or hot-glue gun.

When I was eight or nine, there was this off-the-wall, out-of-control kid from my school. He was a mess behavior-wise, sort of like the bully Sid from *Toy Story*, but weirder. Still, my mom knew his mom from church, and there was no father around, so she felt compelled to reach out to the two of them. Unfortunately, that meant she often saddled me with this kid.[6] I did the best I could with him, but one

---

6 I feel bad telling a story about my mom like this out of context, but it was the truth, and she was just doing the best she could to be a good neighbor and a good Christian. Years later, she understood the impact of this kid, and we made peace with it, so it's okay.

afternoon when he was invited over, he broke my slot car race track and laughed with delight at his destructive accomplishment. That night, my dad put the track in the anvil vise and glued it back together. It wasn't adjustable anymore, but that was fine, and my dad made sure that kid didn't visit anymore.

There's a certain security knowing that there are things that exist that are essentially unbreakable. So many things in life can be so easily erased, cracked, broken, and replaced, and that's life, but everyone should have something immutable to rely on. After all, a good anvil fears no hammer.[7]

I miss that anvil. I wish we would have taken it when we sold the house, with the few other things we kept, but it's sort of like a pool table—it usually stays with the house once it's in, so I guess that stays in the past. It's probably still in the basement with the new owners of the house. I wonder if it will outlive them as well.

---

7 German and Italian proverb.

SCIENCE PROJECT

*You teach me, I forget. You show me, I
remember. You involve me,
I understand.*

—Edward O. Wilson

1986

The trope of parents doing the work of school science projects for their kids is nearly an American institution. It has made it through generations of sitcom plots. A Google or IMDb search will reveal many predictable laugh-track-enhanced scenes of a frazzled, exhausted mother or father up half the night finishing these projects, either out of desperation to get them done so their child will not fail or out of extension of their out-of-control ego to prove that their child is "smart." I'm glad my family dodged that cliché. For my dad, science projects were just another way for him to be around and do what came easily to him—sharing his enthusiasm of doing things well.

My sister, Jean, and I went to the same tiny Lutheran kindergarten through eighth grade school in Des Plaines, Illinois, for much of my childhood. She's four years older than me, so when I was in second or third grade, she was in sixth or seventh. All the kids in sixth, seventh, and eighth grades got to do science projects for the annual school science fair.

Because my dad was involved, I remember Jean's science projects. The first one she did was called "Is It Clear?" The experiment was to determine what type of water made the clearest ice cubes—tap water, distilled, boiled, or bottled. I took an interest because they used a photo sensor from my junior electronics experiment set to measure how much light went through an ice cube. For a few nights, on the kitchen table, Jean and Dad set up some ice cubes, frozen from different water sources, on my mom's clear kitchen cutting board, which they suspended over the sensor from the kit, marking down the light transmission results from a new batch of cubes each evening.

There was another experiment, "Red Hot Heat," where the two of them mounted a hardware-store heat-lamp bulb on a frame of two-by-fours to see how distance from the heat source affected a thermometer. I think it might have been a convenient excuse for my dad to build something with two-by-fours since there was no decorative or desk-lamp body that could hold this odd-shaped bulb.

Then there was the tasty one—"Let It Rise"—in which Jean and Dad experimented with different water temperatures when adding yeast to dough and seeing how fluffy the bread came out.

By age eight I had already managed to annoy my sister in every way possible, so when I found out she was going to do a science project one year, I decided I had to do a science project too, even though I was too young to enter the fair. I don't recall the details of the argument I made, but I think my parents finally said I could do one and it might or might not be displayed at the school, so I was happy with that.

Finding some project I could do as an eight-year-old was the next challenge. My dad came up with the idea of probability—"Why don't you test how likely you are to choose something at random?" When I asked what that meant, he said, "Well, if you have five black balls and five red balls in a bag and choose one with your eyes closed, what color do you think you'll pull out?" I told him that it would probably be red about half the time and black half the time. "Well, you could do an experiment and prove it."

So I took over my mom's sewing table (this wasn't a workshop project) and got started with annoying my sister with my imitation antics for a few days.[8] I went through all the steps in the instructions for her own science project. I had to create a hypothesis, describe an experiment, collect data, then draw a conclusion, and of course, present it all on a large white poster board.

I started out with a set of red and white checkers from my dad's chess set box, put them into a cloth bag, and started the trials of taking out one at a time. I was doing all right, until about halfway through the hundred trials I decided on, when two checkers stuck together and came out at once. I quickly said, "Oh, I'll put that one back."

"Nope—we have to scrap this experiment and try something new," my dad replied.

"But what does it matter? Both checkers were the same color," I protested.

"What if next time you get one of each? It's not a fair trial. We need to find something new where this can't happen," he said with a frown.

---

8 In reality, my sister Jean is enormously patient and accepting, but I am certain that at eight years old, I managed to wear on most people, so it's a reflection on me, not her.

Science Project

I wasn't too happy about starting over, but I went along with the new plan. We happened to have some small red and black plastic balls from my dad's workshop, and they definitely couldn't stick together, so I started the experiment over with those, and I eventually had that data sheet that proved that indeed, if you pull a ball out of a bag of five black and five red balls over and over, it will be black close to half the time.

Though reasonably correct, all the written material from the project was still obviously done by a messy but determined child—it looked like the "Can Spiders Talk to Cats?" experiment from the "Flowers for Charlie" episode of *It's Always Sunny in Philadelphia.* Still, the school put it on display in a corner and gave me a little participation ribbon at the fair, and that was enough for me.

What a way to grow up! To have a parent who wanted their children to strive for the best but had nothing to prove personally, so they could be a friendly guide, not an obsessive stage parent. I'll elaborate later, but my dad did not have the same comfortable childhood full of opportunity I enjoyed. How did he manage to be so involved as a parent without a chip on his shoulder? I fall short of that sometimes. What was his secret?

LEPRECHAUN DETECTOR

> *I am enough of the artist to draw freely*
> *upon my imagination. Imagination*
> *is more important than knowledge.*
> *Knowledge is limited. Imagination*
> *encircles the world.*
> —Albert Einstein

1986

My dad's silly, creative side caught most people off guard. His source of ideas came from nowhere, like magic.

At family gatherings, he would create an Easter-egg-like hunt of animal tracks in the yard with a garden spade and ask my two young cousins to guess what type of real or fictional animal made them—a large chicken, a dinosaur, maybe some sort of yeti or Sasquatch, or even a hungry ostrich?

At my aunt and uncle's house or at the family

cabin, after lunch he'd perfectly time an innocent observation. "Anna, I'm not sure, but I saw something strange in the mud out back. Something has been here—I don't know what. Could you take a look?" With that the hunt would begin.

For my sister, Dad wrote a series of adventures about our two cats, personifying them as being lords of a castle and indulging in their lazy, snuggly, snack-oriented lifestyle. Watching him attempt to type out descriptive prose at a solid six words per minute was endearing—it wasn't his strong suit, but he kept at it until he had a small collection of cat tales.

For me, Dad told the most amazing bedtime stories when I was little—they would often involve a young child who discovered a mysterious world but couldn't take anything back with him to show their friends it existed, or maybe a magical factory that made toys, but it made toys specific to what the child who entered the factory would like—his ideas could rival the world of Harry Potter.

Once, my dad came along for a school trip when I was eight. It was Saint Patrick's Day—the school had a picnic and some outdoor event at a botanical garden. What might my dad do to help out on a trip like this? Build a leprechaun detector, of course! Earlier, my dad and I had found some old industrial plastic housing in the workshop—like something you'd pull off the shoulder joint of Robocop or Iron Man. Inside this empty case, Dad bolted a loud mechanical push-button switch—probably a broken override switch for an electric garage door opener or something similar, but it made a loud and satisfying click when you pressed it. After drilling a hole in the plastic case, he inserted some electrical house wiring, kept partially inside by the switch, with the rest extending out a few inches. The key element to this design was that he could hold this device in his hands and secretly tuck a finger into the hollow space, where he could click the switch and wiggle the "antenna" on the device when a "leprechaun" was nearby. A green LED lit up with a battery, and a small shamrock sticker finished the device—the whole thing could have passed as a prop from the 1960s *Star Trek*.

At the class picnic on a dull, gray day in Chicago in March, the faculty didn't plan anything special at the garden, and eight-year-olds can only be enthralled by the wonders of foliage for so long.

Sensing this, my dad quietly spoke to one of my classmates. "I heard there were leprechauns in the area, but I'm not sure . . . Have you seen anything suspicious?"

I'm sure the kid didn't know what to say but gathered my dad was counting on him for key intel on this question. Then Dad then showed him, and a few other children who had gathered around, this black plastic, high-tech-looking gizmo.[9] He let the children in on his plan. "I built this device to detect leprechauns—let's see if it tells us anything." He powered on the LED light and swept the small crowd of children, leading with the "antenna." Suddenly, as the antenna pointed toward one boy, it started wiggling, and we could hear a clicking—slower, then faster, like a Geiger counter. As he moved closer toward the child, the clicking quickened, and the children laughed (thankfully, the boy being "detected" laughed as well) and ran in different directions. Dad entertained the entire class all afternoon with this stunt and never revealed his secret or what he had found, simply saying, "Well, we don't know—there could be a leprechaun here. Maybe it's someone close by."

The next day at school, a boy from my class approached me, as he was still fascinated by yesterday's

---

9 My dad did not live to see the massive rise of the smartphone. I'm sure he would have loved it and would have developed all sorts of apps to help with carpentry and forestry, but there is a small bittersweet notion that the era of gizmos and gadgets is mostly behind us, all replaced by the convenient, sterile conformity of an app-store-approved smartphone app. I'm not a luddite—I never stand in the way of efficiency and progress—but a leprechaun-detecting "app" just doesn't sound like much fun.

performance. "Steve, I have to know—I know there's no such thing as leprechauns, but how did your dad's detector work? How did it do that?"

I couldn't resist the appeal of the magic. I did not let him in on the gimmick's secret.

I'll never know the full extent to how my dad got his ideas or what he encountered as he developed them. Who knows what the Lutheran school staff said about the leprechaun detector? They probably weren't a fan of *Ghostbusters*. One related thing I learned decades later is that the school staff was not crazy about Halloween either and discouraged kids from dressing up in costumes. My mom and dad never told me this, though, and encouraged me to dress up anyway. One of my favorite costumes was a space alien with all sorts of wiring and electronics coming out of his space helmet—Dad obviously helped with that one too.

What a joy it is to look back and remember a parent who understood harmless, creative fun should be nurtured. To know that even someone with a Christian background could learn to say "Take it easy. It's just pretend." Could I have asked for a better example growing up?

THE COMPASS

*I'm limited by the technology
of my time, but one day you'll figure
this out. And when you do,
you will change the world.*

—Howard Stark, *Iron Man 2*

1994

We all have limits—we can only do so much on our own. We need a hammer, a blade, a lever, or some other artifact of the shoulders of genius to help us on our way. My dad understood this, so he owned a lot of tools.

I have a few of my dad's tools framed in shadow boxes up on the wall in my hidden-away basement office area at home. There's his Swiss Army knife, which he carried with him every day for decades and fixed countless toys, games, and household items with. There's his soldering gun—probably sixty years old now—the main tool for so much of what he did in his workshop for building and fixing electronics. There's a TV remote he designed in the seventies— one of my earliest childhood memories is using it with our family TV when I was little.

The folks at the frame shop have learned to recognize me from everything they've helped me display and preserve. These wall hangings, along with his 1950s multimeter, patent certificates, and a few old books make up a small engineering museum I've curated over the years. It's my version of the man cave. It's more of a man corner, but I love it—it's my favorite part of the house and the one area I keep neat and tidy, right next to my work desk, where the neatness and tidiness end abruptly.

My most treasured item that made it up on the wall is my dad's compass set. From around 1960, it came in a green felt-lined box with a vinyl cover—a much sturdier case than the ziplock bag most drawing supplies come in today. The compass was a non-spring-loaded bow design with a precise thumbwheel to open and close it. The set included dividers, a steel can of graphite leads, and some pen and pencil extension rods.

When I took pre-calc and calculus in high school,

the teacher told me I needed to get a bow compass, so we bought one from OfficeMax, and it was about the only model you could buy anywhere. Though better than the compasses that just held position with friction, you could still tell the device was cheap. It wiggled and slid around as you used it—the pieces still barely fit together. Even as a teenager, I saw that this tool had a short lifespan ahead of it.

After a few months, my dad apparently couldn't take looking at the less-than-flawless arcs and circles I was drawing for much longer, so he let me do my homework with his drafting tools.

Of course, this meant my dad watched my schoolwork more closely. My dad was messy, like me, with horrible handwriting, like me as well, but to his credit he was at least an organized messy person (I never even made it that far), so he scolded me for the rest of my homework looking like a crime scene even if the arcs and lines were neat. He could be a bit of a taskmaster—it wore on me, but the lines and curves stay in my mind.

The days of my dad scrutinizing my math homework came to an end eventually. After I went away to college, I was overwhelmed with challenges a thousandfold greater than high school, and while I did still draw, it was mostly on the computer, where I eventually built my career in computer drawing and graphics. The compass set was lost and forgotten somewhere in our home for years.

A month or two after my dad died and I was able to think about everyday things again with some clarity, I had a moment of panic. If I could have just one thing from the house—just one . . . Where was it!? The next time I flew home, I searched the workshop, the computer room, through piles and piles of papers and books, until I saw a hint of green vinyl from under some manila envelopes in a filing cabinet. I felt relief and hugged the compass case. I knew I had to go right to the frame shop before I lost it again.

I didn't realize this until after I put it up on the wall behind glass, but what made my dad's compass better specifically wasn't obvious. It wasn't so much that it didn't have a gap or seam out of place—that was certainly part of it—but the main difference was the weight. It had a lot of extra solid steel in strategic places to make it stable. With a heavier drawing tool, you can gently drag a line, not press. Pressing causes wiggles and shifts in the pencil. It's just like when I would saw beams in the workshop—placing my full weight into the task and getting the saw jammed in the wood. My dad told me once, "Don't press down. The saw is sharp. Let the saw and the weight of the saw do the work."

It's almost impossible to buy fine drawing tools like this anymore. You can come close, but the market just isn't there for making smooth, consistent lines and curves by hand anymore. I tried—I wanted to get a compass for my niece, and I found something nice but not quite what I was hoping for. I normally don't jump on the "They don't make them like they used to" bandwagon, but in this case, it's true. If you do find a quality tool, though, of any kind, working with it rather than against it will be what matters most.

Tools have a special place in my family. Largely because of when I was born, with modern tools like software, I have the opportunity to do so much more than my dad and his dad could. Will I achieve my full potential with these tools just as they did with theirs? Will anyone?

TALKING

A word is worth one coin—
silence is worth two.

—The Talmud

1990

Recently, on a lazy Saturday afternoon, when my wife and daughter were out of town, I saw part of the movie *Jarhead*. There was one scene with a drill sergeant and a recruit that went something like this:

"Did your dad serve in Vietnam?!"

"Sir, yes, sir!"

"Did he ever talk about it?!"

"Sir, only once, sir!"

"Good. Then he wasn't lying!"

This literally gave me pause—I stopped the movie and thought for a few minutes. I eventually finished it, but I continued to think for a couple days, and I finally concluded that my dad never—even once—talked about his childhood. I don't think he ever talked about his mother. He talked about college sometimes, which was always a good time, but that was it. It was an odd void in his personality for someone so involved with his own family.

No matter where I looked, there was simply almost nothing to see about my dad, nothing to hear. Once, when I was ten, I found an old photo of me in a box in the dark, unfinished part of basement next to our spare light bulbs. It was strange. I did not recognize where it was taken, and I was wearing this ugly sweater I had never seen. What was also strange was that my great-uncle Ed, standing beside me, looked so young and healthy. There was also a tin of copper BBs in the box. I had a BB gun, but I knew they'd stopped making BBs out of copper a long time ago, and they certainly didn't come in metal tins anymore. That's when I realized the obvious. Why this picture was never in any of our family albums, I can only guess. I never saw another like it.

I only know a few details of my dad's childhood (from my mom). My dad's dad, Walter Mycynek, died of pneumonia when Dad was about ten months old. Mom said that Walter could have possibly lived with the right treatment, but the newer, more effective sulfur-based antibiotics he needed while ill were all going overseas to the troops fighting the Nazis in World War II.[10] Dad's older sister, my aunt, was born mentally handicapped, and his mom wasn't in the best of health either and died when Dad was in his early twenties.

Despite all this, my dad wasn't some closed-off alcoholic Red Forman / Great Santini type. On the contrary, he was a wonderful individual who gave love and was loved, but anything about growing up poor, being on food stamps, and taking care of his sister never came up. Even my mom nervously reminded me sometimes that "he never talks about it." It's possible he just didn't think it was important, but with all the things he did consider important, this was hard to believe.

There were a few clues about the silence that I see only in retrospect. When I was eleven, I loved 1950s oldies like "Rock Around the Clock," probably after seeing *Back to the Future* or *Happy Days*. I asked my dad if he liked fifties music when he was a kid, and he replied that he didn't because it was "too sad." "Rock Around the Clock" too sad? My preadolescent mind

---

10 Today, in the 2020s, when people get resentful about the COVID-19 vaccine or having to wear a mask, I usually have a few strong words for them.

was dumfounded.

Another time, we all went to a retro fifties-style restaurant for dinner. It must have been my mom's idea. This place was a re-creation, not an original, but it had the usual memorabilia cranked up a little too loudly, meatloaf and string beans, ice cream sodas, neon signs, waitresses on roller skates, and the like.

We survived the meal without incident, but my dad was bewildered by the whole evening and exclaimed, "Why would anyone want to re-create food from that time?"

I didn't understand my dad's reaction to either of these 1950s experiences, but now, it's clear there was no Norman Rockwell painting of my dad following the jolly postman carrying bundles of Christmas presents to a lucky child's home.

Even given the perfect opportunity and a prop, my dad still didn't talk about his youth. His father once carved a chess set out of wood, including the box to hold the pieces, along with some checkers, in 1933, ten years before he was born.

This set looked even more ancient than it was, paint and varnish flaked away, like a ruin recovered from a culture long gone. You could tell it was made partly of household items—tips of clothespins were cut off to make pawns, and the queen crowns were bottle caps—but the rest was sawn and drilled lumber, put together with small brass screws. Two small wooden pockets for decks of playing cards were built into the lid, carefully positioned to not collide with the tops of the pieces when it closed. Given the detail, it must have taken months to build.

My dad taught me to play chess using this set, but he gave no explanation of where it came from. It was the only artifact he had from his childhood, maybe the only thing he owned to connect him to his own father, and the only reason I know that my dad's dad made the set was because he carved his name and the year into the bottom of the box. Like I said, my dad didn't talk about it, and decades later it finally made sense. Action was what could have transformed his early life, not words. Therefore, his language was action, not words.

Getting back to the *Jarhead* movie . . . if soldiers don't talk about war because it was just that horrible, just how bad was life for my dad growing up?

It makes me wonder more about the life experiences we hear about versus don't hear about. Some people are all too keen on telling you their traumatic stories about high school, adolescence, and heartbreak, and while I don't want to dismiss that, should we instead press others to talk about what they never volunteer, what they keep locked away? What could we learn from all that history that was never spoken of? Are we ready to hear it?

SHIRT-BOX GALLERY

I prefer drawing to talking. Drawing is faster, and leaves less room for lies.

—Le Corbusier

1999

My dad, his friend John, and John's cousin Dick were at the University of Wisconsin–Madison, studying electrical engineering in the mid-sixties. John's girlfriend, Carol, was studying nursing at the University of Wisconsin–Milwaukee and later the University of Hawaii, as was her best friend and roommate, Marion.

One day Carol and Marion were near a fire station, and they asked some fireman to take their picture sitting on a fire truck. Carol sent John the picture. My dad saw the picture of Carol and Marion and abruptly asked John, "Who is that other person? Could I write to her?" About twelve years later, I knew Marion better as "Mom." Thank God the fire department just let people wander in and take photos back then.

John and Carol, their kids, and Dick's kids were my family's oldest friends and a fixture in our traditions. Every Fourth of July and New Year's, our families would celebrate together. Without exception it was barbecues and parades and fireworks in the summer and board games, cards, and slide shows in the winter. Dick's son Craig always had the radio on New Year's Eve, listening to the midnight countdown of the top one hundred songs of the year and writing them down in a tiny notebook—such a practice is laughable now, but there was no Google then. These were the jolliest, happiest times of the year— more than Christmas, or Halloween, or my birthday, or the last day of school. Just getting in the car to see John, Carol, Dick, and their kids a few times each year was the most excited I'd get for any occasion.

These holidays were also one of the few times I ever got a peek into my father's past—at least his young adult years. My dad had been at college entirely on student loans and didn't have time to mess around, but he still had a few fun memories from that era in his life.

While we took turns showing off the many carousels of slides from decades past, there were lots of stories about my dad and his friends stealing one another's snacks or arguing over *Star Trek* versus *Lost in Space,* to which my dad would say, "Oh, I couldn't stand that Dr. Smith." Granted, my dad saw a lot in life that caused many somber streaks in his psyche, but these are the times when we'd hear him guffaw and remind everyone of the time that Dick tried to label an individual egg or radish in the refrigerator, or they'd try to figure out what kind of blanket or sheet was best to use as a makeshift tent to shield the lamp brightness in the dorm room when one person was studying and one was sleeping. I never specifically wished my dad were more like other dads, but it was still nice to see him go on a bit about more everyday things that made him happy.

My favorite story my dad told was about an interior decorating tradition he and John and Dick had at the house they'd rented after graduation. Back then men's shirts came in those cheap, thin cardboard boxes you might still occasionally see, and men still wore collared shirts most of the time. My dad and his friends had a few of these boxes lying around, so they came up with the idea that anyone who visited their rental house had to draw a picture on a shirt box, and they would then hang that picture on the wall with the others from previous guests. Knowing my dad, I'm sure these were silly, cartoon-like drawings. Allegedly they were mostly doodles of frustrations with landlords, car trouble, term papers—all the usual gripes and stressors of a typical twentysomething. This was his version of the *Animal House* toga party.

When you say that out loud, it sounds tacky and silly, and it is, but I tried the same thing in college with my roommates. When people would visit our run-down three-bedroom apartment at the University of Illinois, they'd look at the wall covered with six-foot rolls of black construction paper (classy!), and we'd hand our new guest a yellow pad and instruct them to "Draw something. If you're not sure what to draw, draw something that frustrates you." We received pictures of snowstorms, broken furniture, people stood up on dates, horrible professors, and malfunctioning washing machines, but also some palm trees, Garfield the cat, a painfully detailed rendering of the crucifixion of Jesus,[11] and plenty of other gems.

This practice was an unbelievable hit—we easi-

---

11 How someone took the instructions of "Draw something that frustrates you" and took that to mean "Spend forty-five minutes doing a shaded perspective view of a hand nailed to a board, blood dripping down to the bottom of the page, with the caption "Daily" was beyond me—maybe the forgiveness of Jesus Christ really ruined his day.

ly got a hundred drawings up on that wall, and we were not popular guys to begin with. It got to the point where I wasn't even the chief gallery evangelist anymore—my roommates would help curate the yellow-pad museum with new pieces if I wasn't there.

Being a young generation Xer, I was often discouraged by how annoyed and dismissive my generation was of everything at that age. Everything was lame, everything was a sell-out, everyone was a poseur. It was hard to do much of anything without someone finding fault with it and claiming it wasn't "real." For once, though, this was different. I could not believe that a typical too-cool-for-school twenty-year-old would embrace this, but it brought people together, which I needed at the time. There's something to be said about giving people license to create their own graffiti. Because we kept it up for years and accepted it as part of our house, this probably struck a chord with a lot of people who just wanted to be heard, even if what they were saying wasn't all that profound.

Today, inclusion and giving people a voice is a big issue in America. While that's possibly easier said than done, getting into the spirit of listening to and lifting up others could start with simple acts like this.

RAY

All faults may be forgiven of him who
has perfect candor
—Walt Whitman

1989

I'm grateful my parents were good people first and good Christians second. This distinction came out in candid, natural ways.

Being his candid, natural self, my dad would tell me bits and pieces of trivia about television and electronics from work. Every day at any time, he'd throw in an aside about some chip or board or circuit that was or wasn't doing what it should, something about square waves and compression and other tidbits relating to analog and digital television signals, all somehow related to a tangent earlier in the conversation in a way only he focused on. Once, while taking a cookie from a cookie sheet on the table after dinner, he remarked that "TV antennas of the future will be thin metal sheets." This was almost thirty-five years ago, but take a look at TV antennas and their shapes on Amazon.com today, and you'll see his tangents had merit.

That's what his stream of consciousness was like.

One name that often came up in these jumbles of story fragments was Ray.

Ray was a technician at my dad's workplace. He would take my dad's circuit board designs and solder them together, sometimes using chips my dad and others designed, and test them out. We didn't know much about Ray compared to Dad's other work friends we'd see sometimes—Ray was a more casual acquaintance. As a kid with an overactive imagination, I filled in some details and guessed he was like a friendly bit-part character I'd see in my favorite sitcom, and I envisioned him coming into a scene at the office as a foil to my dad and delivering some one-line zinger that would cue the laugh track. The story of Ray didn't continue that way though.

The late eighties were a scary time because of one word: AIDS. Depending on how old you are, AIDS is either a footnote or something up there with COVID-19 and school shootings, but back then people were terrified, and rightfully so—there were barely any treatments.

As AIDS crept more and more into the news, politics, religion, school curriculum, and every aspect of life, I still felt like it was something mostly other, older people had to worry about, but that didn't stop it from coming up in conversation at least a couple times a week somewhere in most people's days.

When I was eleven, one night after dinner we were all in our usual spots in the living room around the TV. As we were settling down to relax for the evening, I asked my dad what was going on at Zenith, and he suddenly became serious as he told the family that Ray had AIDS.

This topic was already awkward, and my dad was not exactly the president of the local Toastmasters. Still, he gathered up the stamina to say, "Ray's not doing too well with AIDS." When we asked more, he said "Well, I don't know, but I think he's bisexual—I've heard him mention his wife at home and also some guy on the side. I don't really know."

I was out of my element here, so I just listened as my dad told more. He wasn't comfortable with the situation, and I could see a serious struggle in his mind. He wore this look of hurt and confusion, which was understandable, but he managed to squeeze out a few more words. "I told Ray that it's not too late, and he should do whatever he needs to do to make things okay. Jesus was always open to him, or if he had some other religion, they certainly could help him too, but he should do something to make sure he's okay." My dad was straining to muster even that much detail.

In 2023 the social and political tarpit of society's views on boomer mentality has exhausted us all, and while I don't like to gloss over the past with "that's just how it was back then," even the most enlightened of us are a product of our times, and we too will all look narrow minded to our own children and grandchildren twenty or fifty years from now. My dad did the best he could, being born in 1943 and raised Catholic, at a time when even the president wore gloves when meeting AIDS patients. He mentioned several times over the years that gays "are people" and that "I think they're born that way," and I could see the gears turning in his head trying to reconcile his kind, decent, common-sense nature with something that a lifetime of traditional values didn't recognize.

I suspect that often my dad's less-than-stellar speaking and communication skills were an asset and not a liability. It was not possible for him to be anything other than himself, so while suggesting "Look into Jesus or someone similar and do what you need to do" in this case might have been the best or most politically correct advice, the fact that he cared so deeply despite being conflicted is what came through—no matter what he said, that always came through. I've continued that quirk, maybe with too much enthusiasm. My wife will attest that my pursuit of truth and sincerity too often comes come out as a series of crazy non sequiturs that I've struggled to rein in for decades. No one embodies "it's the thought that counts" quite like me and my dad.

Maybe it was luck, medicine, or even partly my dad reaching out to Ray in the only way he knew how, but Ray lived for quite a while—I finally met him at my dad's funeral years later. He was thin, his eyes sunken far into his skull, but he was there. When he introduced himself, all the memories of that time years ago came back. I'll never know exactly what else my dad said to Ray or how he said it, but it was enough for him to come visit us years later when we were in need.

Common advice states that "silence is golden," or "if you're not sure what to say, don't say anything." While refraining from comment in difficult situations may save you embarrassment, I always remember doing the contrary sometimes is worth the risk.

BUYING THE ROAD

*Without property rights, no other
rights are possible.*

—Ayn Rand

1972

Some of my dad's big interests were trees, forests, and woodworking. I'll admit I didn't appreciate nature the way he did. I didn't like the heat, the humidity, the bugs, and the allergies. I hated putting on bug spray and sunscreen and wearing heavy clothes to protect from ticks. It just wasn't me. I can tell you the difference between a pine and a spruce (we were firmly a "spruce" family when it came to Christmas trees), but that's about as far as I get into understanding trees. My dad, on the other end of the spectrum, had a large hardcover book on forestry titled

The International Book of Wood, by Hugh Johnson.[12] As a teenager, my friends and I laughed ourselves silly whenever we saw this book on his shelf. Anyway, he loved trees—you get it. And even though his passion for trees was exhausting sometimes, I could always hear in his voice how important they were to him, so I knew better than to rain on his parade. One of his last projects before he died was a forest survey multi-tool made of PVC pipe, string, strategically placed metal screws, and a small compass. It could measure tree height, age, cubic feet of lumber per acre, and a few other things with some math and geometry tricks. He made a dozen of them to give away at the next Wisconsin woodland owners association meeting he was attending. A T-shirt with a phrase printed on it we got him once explained him best: "If you wish to be happy for a year, plant a garden. If you wish to be happy for a lifetime, plant a tree."

Trees were a big part of my family from long before I was born. Though he liked the Green Bay Packers, Dad wasn't a sports fanatic—he was too lanky for most games and wasn't a competitive person. Growing up, he didn't have the money or time to be into cars. My guess is that trees had a certain timeless beauty that didn't need a schedule or maintenance, like baseball season or a classic Corvette. In the early seventies,

---

12 As Dave Barry would say, "I am not making this up."

after he finally had some money of his own, my dad bought 120 acres of undeveloped forest land in Wisconsin. It was three forty-acre parcels with a creek running through it and lots of trees (though some clearing too), just off a long country road. He probably bought that location because it was a few miles away from my mom's extended family's cabin, where we'd all spend a week or two in the summer. It was technically a young forest—even now the trees are barely tall enough to harvest for lumber. My dad spent as much time as he could there, watching the trees grow, planting new ones, cutting away brush to make trails, and making maps of them. He even named two trees there after my sister and me, pointing them out whenever we walked or drove by, saying, "There's your tree, Steven, and there's Jean's."

To say this land was remote would be an understatement. The most obvious clue was the insect noise. Locusts and cicadas were all you could hear, and given the absence of everything else that could make a sound, they seemed unusually loud, to the point where I never got used to it. The summer heat in central Wisconsin is unbearable—add in humidity, waist-high grass and weeds, and insects that sounded like disgruntled Metallica roadies with dental drills in the distance—and you had to really love nature to want to be out there.

The only reason, as a proud indoor kid, that I tolerated any of this was that this was where my dad and I would launch our model rockets when I was nine or ten. It was an exercise in preparation, since once we were out there, we wouldn't want to be stuck without batteries, tape, water, and other supplies, but I toughed it out and made it there just to have a chance to see those rockets go off into the sky and have enough empty space to chase after them and hopefully retrieve them. We'd usually take a dozen or so I'd built in the past year—most would survive, but a few are probably still a hundred feet up a pine tree somewhere there today. It was probably the most exercise I'd get all year.

The land was about a quarter mile in from the main road. My dad wasn't a real estate expert, but simply having a legal right to pass through someone else's land to get to his wasn't good enough. Rather than take his chances with easement laws that would hopefully allow him to come and go as he pleased, he decided to buy an additional strip of land leading into his 120 acres from the main road as well. He even bought a width twice as much as he'd need for a vehicle to allow for drainage and wide loads. "Two rods wide, because I might need the extra room taking the van over that uncut area," he said.[13] Eventu-

13 One rod is about 16.5 feet.

ally he built this area into a gravel road with a gate so we'd always have a way into it.

It's been years since I've visited this land. I'd need to take at least two flights and rent a car just to see it, especially now that my mom's family doesn't have a home near there anymore. As much as I fill my time with hobbies and interests, this is one thing I've mostly let go. My sister and I will eventually decide what to do with it, but for now, it stays put—I don't think either of us has the emotional reserve right now to make any plans regarding it.

Even though I don't think about the land much, the part that sticks with me is going through the extra trouble and expense of buying, building, and maintaining the road into it. He told me about the road often enough, but the reason went over my head when I was younger. Why all the extra effort on owning his own road to his land? I suspect that growing up, my dad had his share of disappointments where despite his best efforts, being poor and without opportunity left him close to what he wanted but not quite there. I am sure he was on the losing end of "life isn't fair" or "what might be your right on paper is not necessarily what you get" more than he'd care to remember.

Access, whether the road is real or metaphorical, is part of privilege. How many people in America who grow up without privilege get the access to affordable health care, school lunch programs, or other things they are allegedly entitled to? So when Dad had the means, he made the extra investment to be prepared, to make sure that what was his would always be his and his children's—no exceptions. That spirit of being prepared and being grateful I have the means to be prepared stays with me. It's tedious at times—just look at how many spare cell phone batteries I pack on a trip—but when I have access to what I need exactly when I need it, I think back to my dad's road.

PAUSE

Well done is better than well said.
—Ben Franklin

2004

It's inaccurate to say my dad didn't talk. He wasn't a big talker, because he was busy doing, and he didn't talk about his childhood, but he wasn't unusually shy. One quirk of his speech still echoes in my mind, even this very moment. When my dad spoke, his speech was filled with unexpected pauses, followed by some oddly specific noun, adjective, adverb, or analogy. He was like William Shatner, the way he'd break up a sentence into the most unexpected fragments.

Other people noticed this too—he had a distinct diction, and my friends mentioned it enough that I used to do this impression of what him giving me the facts-of-life talk would be like.[14] It would have gone something like this: "Steve . . . Sometimes when you put . . . . . . two things . . . together . . . a . . . . . . third party . . . is . . . yielded . . . that was not part of the original . . . . scenario . . . and this can have an effect on your . . . . 1040-A." I lit up the room with this impression more than a few times.[15]

I didn't understand the reason for my dad's speech until I was much older, out of college, and more aware of how similar we were. When my dad spoke, you could see how hard he was thinking—

---

14 I could write another book filled with stories about my mom, as she was a school nurse, so she brought home all the books and movies about puberty the school would give to and show the students in health class (to review them for quality and age appropriateness). Given that my mom couldn't work the VCR, I saw dozens of these "What's happening to my body" videos with her and had my own Roger Ebert-like critique of each one down to a science by the time I was done with junior high. "Thumbs down on using pancake batter on a griddle to illustrate the ovaries and fallopian tubes—you'll get so many laughs the kids will miss the point" was my review on one of them.

15 Another joke based on a real conversation with my dad goes like this: Jesus and my dad are shopping at Kmart. My dad gets some Planters peanuts, and Jesus gets some memory cards for his digital camera. They then come to the paper goods aisle, and my dad says, "Oh, I need some paper towels." <Pause> "Tell me, Jesus. What do you think influences the absorbency of paper towels more? <Pause> The distance between the dimples in the paper towel sheet <Pause> or the diameters of the dimples themselves?" And Jesus says, "Just buy whatever the hell is on sale!"

trying to get the exact idea out at any cost, and if it took longer, oh well. To be clear, he did not have a stutter or a speech impediment, and he wasn't trying to sound scholarly or dramatic, like a Shakespeare monologue—he was just absolutely determined to get his message out properly when he was speaking. The fact that he worked so hard that he seemed strained was a window into how much respect he had for whom he was speaking with.

It has been said that "tragedy plus time equals comedy." Many great comedians have had great pain, and with time and insight they've managed to transform it into something else. My dad was the same way. He spoke with such intention that the result was an accurate truth told in a way that could make you laugh, even if that wasn't what he was going for. Others also picked up on this. Who did the Zenith social committee call on when they wanted someone to speak at a retirement dinner? My dad. He'd have a way of retelling tales with embarrassing accuracy that brought out the humanity and humility of the time he and his coworkers spent together. When my aunt Ruth and uncle Rudy got married, he wrote a best-man speech full of jokes and puns about their shared interests that was so silly but delivered in such a way that you knew every word was true. He spoke of their love of bicycling and how their parents couldn't wait to "peddle these two off." All the pauses in the delivery didn't hurt either.

I unknowing inherited my dad's "Shatner speak" and learned about this at the most unexpected time. At my dad's visitation and funeral, there were coworkers of his I hadn't met, and after greeting them and talking to them for a minute, one remarked, "He's got the same way of talking, the same mannerisms, the same gestures." The others nodded in agreement. This man was much older, with thick glasses and bushy gray eyebrows. Behind all the age, I could see the faintest look of fear in his eyes while making this comparison, as if he had seen a ghost.

In the years that followed, more people noticed they could not just see but hear the gears turning when I thought or listened. Some people have even wondered if they'd offended me in conversation because of how I'd pause and give a funny look at the worst possible times, and I had to reassure them. "It's not you! It's just how I think!" It was not an ideal trait for the dating scene as a young man.

It wasn't all bad though. Looking back on my earliest childhood memories, I internalized that letting people see your thought process, even if it was messy, was a sign of honor and integrity, and people responded to it. When I was eight, I wanted to tell jokes in the school talent show, and the music teacher in charge, probably picking up on my personality, suggested I be the master of ceremonies instead, introducing each act and maybe saying something funny along with it. I don't know how, but I took that and ran. With enormous thought and pausing, I found a way to joke about each act while being endearing but not mocking to the cast. At the beginning I even came out and did a Johnny Carson–like mic check and then yelled back, "Yeah, it works" behind the curtain. Somehow I knew that being clumsy about breaking the fourth wall was my way of saying "I'm not a professional, but hey, let's all have some fun together anyway."

Years later I did some stand-up comedy at a few open mics in Boston and even got invited back for a few special events. I proudly once earned six dollars, so I guess I'm technically a pro. Stand-up comedy is a grueling lifestyle—lots of Wednesday and Thursday nights up till 1:30 a.m. eating bar food when you need to be at work the next day—so my time on stage is rare these days, but my formula of being painfully specific, even if it's painful for the audience as they wait for the rest of the sentence, was the basis for my act, but it wasn't really "acting" in the strictest sense.

Even off the comedy stage, my public speaking is a little unpolished, but I've come to celebrate it. I have a variation of a speech I give at all my wife's cousin's weddings based on my own experience becoming part of the family. I didn't even realize that I was continuing my dad's tradition until recently.

I often speak of how I just can't help myself—I have to be the way that I am. Sometimes I wish I were more graceful—a smooth talker, but if I had the chance, I wouldn't have changed how my dad was, so I've learned to embrace the pause.

THE NEXT LEVEL

*Teach for the future; you have to live
in it.*
—Bjarne Stroustrup

1992

My dad didn't have a ton of grand theories or proverbs about life. Instead, I laugh imagining him picking up a copy of *Life's Little Instruction Book* with a pair of needle-nose pliers, peering at a random platitude from it, frowning, and carefully placing the book deep in the back of a drawer, where it might never see the light of day again. There is an exception though. One thing my dad said about education was that you often need to go one level beyond what you need in your everyday life to use what you do need effectively. To use something or do something well, you often need to know the theory of how it works and how that inner working is applied to your daily situation.

I think this is lost on many people today who scoff at learning just about anything they don't deem useful. I don't need to speak, read, or write Latin, but I studied so much Latin in high school that whenever I see French, Spanish, or Italian, about half the time I can see a root or hear a sound hinting at what the word means. For example, the French word for "computer," *ordinateur*, can be broken down to "ordinal" —> *number* and "ateur" —> *one who does* —> number doer —> number machine —> computer. I'm hardly an expert linguist, but for a dead language, Latin has many live applications.

My dad's favorite example was math. Algebra helped you master arithmetic. Calculus helped you master algebra.

When people claim that "you'll never use this in real life," the reality is that mostly you may simply never become aware of opportunities to use something you never bothered to learn or how you could use something you learned if you understood it better. This is a little bittersweet, as I sometimes wish I'd gone even farther in school, but at least now I know how knowledge can remove limitations and lack of knowledge can keep them in place.

There was an advertisement for a technical college that ran in the eighties in which some young person was repeatedly turned down for a job because of a lack of education and experience, and the tagline at the end was "What you don't know, can hurt you." My dad knew this. His mom did not want him to go to college—she wanted him to work at the grocery store to help take care of the family, as they were barely getting by. My mom told me how hard it was for my dad to say to his mom, "No. The only way out of poverty is through education," but he did it—he took out loans, he went to school, he finished, and he had everything paid back before I was born (that was possible back then).

My dad's sister stayed behind and washed dishes for decades—it was all she could do given her mental handicap—but my dad set up investments for all her earnings for the past fifty years, so she is still financially secure for life, long after he died.

If my dad had never appreciated the potential from learning more than what he needed to work at a grocery store, who knows how this story would have ended.

Despite his success, I am certain this journey was an enormous burden for my dad when he was young. As I grew older, homework was never easy with my dad. I had an excellent math teacher throughout junior high. He was brilliant and insightful—maybe just a hair too ambitious. He marched us through Algebra 1, 2, and far beyond by the time we were in eighth grade, and it was exhausting. I did well, but it was like CrossFit every day for three years, and when I got home, the CrossFit continued. My dad made sure I got through every problem to his satisfaction. I did well and worked hard, but there were days when it was too much, and I dreaded it. When I'd erase a mistake sloppily, my dad would yell, "Erase it better!" I resented him then more than I like to admit, but I think he feared for me—what would happen to his son if he couldn't do math? What life would he have?

How hard should someone have to work to survive, to thrive? Should everyone experience the fear of poverty, of food stamps, to drive them to do well?

How far beyond the basics do we need to know? Should we know? It's an impossible question to generalize, as not everyone has the same skills, abilities, and interests, but for someone who has felt hunger and cold winters with little relief, it's no wonder they'd push for the harder math classes, the extra years of school, whatever it took, to make sure you had the insight and knowledge to apply yourself and succeed.

FATHER/SON CAMP

*Ladies and gentlemen, I've been
to Vietnam, Afghanistan, and Iraq,
and I can say without hyperbole
that this is a million times worse
than all of them put together.*

—Kent Brockman, "Camp Krusty" from
The Simpsons

1987

My parents did a good job of pushing me to do new things outside my comfort zone without overscheduling me to death with activities, and Cub Scouts was one of them. Cub Scouts was always a mixed bag. I liked it, but maybe not a lot—I wasn't athletic or an outdoor kid, but I loved doing new and interesting things beyond school, so I was willing to put up with a few nature hikes, sing-alongs, and flag football games if it meant I could learn about carpentry, archery, or better ways to light campfires.

The whole family loved campfires. The family cabin in Wisconsin had a small fire pit out back, in a sunken, damp area by a lake. It wasn't conducive for starting fires but was in the safest area for such a thing. One achievement my dad and I had in camp-fires was the twelve-campfire starter kit. This activity was too messy for the workshop, so we went to our second-favorite workspace, the back of the garage by the charcoal grill. We'd take a cardboard egg con-tainer and put three small squares of old T-shirt ma-terial into each egg pocket. Then we'd put some can-dles we got on sale in a Hills Bros. coffee can, light some charcoal in the grill, and melt them down over the fire. The candles were usually pink and purple Advent candles—hence the summer sale—resulting in a strange, unmanly colored mess, but it worked for us, and we'd dump the boiling wax over the egg car-ton. After this all dried, we could then conveniently tear off one of these egg-crate sections and light it. It would burn with an unstoppable, thick, hot bundle of flames for over thirty minutes, long enough to start even the dampest pile of campfire wood. Maybe not patent-pending worthy but still the greatest camping innovation I've ever seen. We convinced the other Scout families that this life hack was the way to go, campfire prep–wise. Consequently, my only camping tip, the actual life hack, is that if you want to get your kids to spend more time outdoors, you'll have more luck baiting them with activities around lighting things on fire than playing "guess the type of moss on this rock."

One summer when I was nine, during peak campfire season at the family cabin, my dad and I decided to take a vacation from our vacation and go to a father-son Cub Scout–sponsored camping trip an hour or two away. It was billed as a week of hiking, boating, swimming, and other outdoor fun. Normally this wouldn't be high on my list of preferred activities, but the camp wasn't too far away, so at least we could sandwich it in with the rest of our time up north. So even though it didn't look like we'd be lighting anything on fire, I was on board for the trip, and my dad and I packed up the car and headed out mid-July to the campground.

It was hot that summer, like it always was in the Midwest, but this was unusual—well over one hundred degrees, with humidity and mosquitoes to boot, for days. No air conditioning, no shade, no chairs, no indoor plumbing—Scouts claim to love these conditions, but I always suspected there was a little "doth protest too much" going on among these camping enthusiasts. I was a little more of a realist. I never did well in the heat, and it was so hot that the lake we swam in was like a warm bath—I didn't know that was possible! Still, we persevered. My dad would often say it was "colder than sin" in the winter. Looking back, I think he said that because he thought it was a bit blasphemous to say "it's hotter than hell" in the summer!

The outdoor fun was just starting. The hot-tub lake wasn't a problem, as I barely got to go into the lake anyway. This was because per Scout policy, we had to swim with the buddy system, and my assigned buddy, some other nine-year-old, didn't want to go in the water. He didn't want to do anything, though he was quite good at whining and yelling at his dad. I can still hear that kid's shrill, bratty voice screaming, "Dad, I want a Coke NOW!" Even then I was embarrassed for both of us. It was amazing to see at that age that I wasn't as far on the indoor/outdoor-kid spectrum as I thought, as I said to myself, *Jeez, I'm a dorky indoor kid and I know it, but this kid makes me look like Indiana Jones.*

At the same time, while I was paired with this buddy for most of the Scouting activities, who carried on like a high-strung cat being taken to the vet, my dad got to go to these new-age fatherhood workshops, where he would learn how to "relate to" and "communicate with" his son. He probably got the worst of the two activity tracks, as from what I overheard him telling my mom, the lectures were apparently put on by self-righteous bearded men who consumed near-fatal doses of pop psychology and then somehow got ahold of a stage and microphone. I can still remember my dad groaning to my mom later on that "they kept going on about 'tuning in' to your son!"

I don't remember too many other details from this camping trip—I doubt there was much that held my interest, as after about thirty-six hours of this, my dad and I, both visibly worn out, gave each other a long, hard look after lunch. Granted, I was nine and I didn't understand cursing, subtext, irony, when it was appropriate to give up, or other adult concepts, but we both knew what the other was thinking, blasphemy aside: "Screw this shit—let's get the hell out of here."

We raced to the car—we didn't even say goodbye to anyone—and I think I saw my dad do seventy on the highway for the first time in my life. We grabbed a few Cokes along the way home.

I guess Dad already knew how to relate to, communicate with, and "tune in to" his son.[16]

---

16 I wanted to end the story with that final one-line sentence, but the message here is simple: Spend time with your kids. Parenting handbooks and seminars are fine, but if they're not your thing, just spend time with your kids, and you'll be fine.

TELEVISION SURVEY

*I think he's trying to watch
some illegal channels!
Honey, that's just bad reception.*

—Mr. and Mrs. Levenstein, *American Pie*

1990

My dad designed television sets and systems for many decades at Zenith Electronics, one of the last American electronics companies that was bought by LG in 1999. One benefit of his job was that he got to take home experimental television prototypes for home evaluation. We'd watch them as our regular family television and then trade them in for a new one each year.

Because of this, television was not just a distraction in our house. It wasn't an addiction, but it wasn't demonized, either, as the reason for the downfall of family values, as was the popular conservative stance back then. Aside from trees and forestry, television was a part of our family culture, no different from barn raising or butter churning for the Amish. My dad and I didn't just "watch" what was on TV—we watched every detail of the television itself. Sharpness, brightness, color saturation, antenna placement. I grew up with a constant discussion of all this.

My dad's ability to simultaneously pay attention and not pay attention to television was hilarious. One time in high school, he had the TV on while doing something else in the workshop, and I asked him what he was watching. "It's this medical show where people come into the hospital with major injuries, but there are also romantic interludes to keep it interesting. I think it's called *ER*." (Probably the most popular show on television in the mid-nineties and the one everyone was constantly talking about.) Another time, when I was watching *The Matrix* when home from college, he sat in his chair reading *Science News* for an entire ninety minutes, then suddenly looked up and remarked, "Oh, I think the fortune-teller lady is going to tell her that she's going to fall in love with whoever is going to be the hero, and she's going to have to make some kind of choice or something."

Hard as it is to believe, I was not very popular at school, but the one home run I could always hit, socially, was bringing in the brochures and catalogs of all the new Zenith products and showing them off to the other kids at lunch—they would drool at all the big screens and new tech catchphrases, like "Dolby," "digital tuning," and "comb filter." One year we got a front-projection TV for home evaluation—they were the size of a dishwasher back then and doubled as a large coffee table—and for my birthday party, we kids got to watch *Back to the Future* on the big screen in our basement. It was nice to be popular once in a great while, and I knew television was something worth holding on to.

Television even went beyond our culture and became our heritage. As a child I proudly thought of television as the "family business." I thought this partly because my dad had worked with his friend Rudy at Zenith since the seventies. In the early eighties, my mom suggested that my dad introduce Rudy to her younger sister Ruth, and that's how he became my uncle Rudy. Years later, whenever we'd visit Aunt Ruth, Uncle Rudy, and my cousins, we'd get to see what TV set they had for home evaluation and talk about the ins and outs of television trends even more.

The most important part of the Zenith home evaluation program was the "evaluation survey."

With each TV came a paper packet—it looked like a standardized test form from school, with instructions to answer multiple choice and essay questions about the TV for Zenith market research.

My dad decided to subcontract this annual duty out to his twelve-year-old son, so I would live for the day each year when I got to fill out a survey rating. Things like—you guessed it—picture sharpness, brightness, color saturation, bass, treble, menu system, and plastic and industrial design choices on a twenty-seven-inch (huge for those days) color TV. One could dismiss his decision as laziness, but my certainly unbiased opinion is that it was a genius research strategy.

How did I proceed with this task? Reruns of *Three's Company* seemed to be on TV all the time when I was twelve. When people use the phrase "misspent youth," I think I could get into a hell of an argument with them over the value of spending a Saturday morning in the basement adjusting the sharpness and contrast on Suzanne Somers and her tight sweaters and then filling out bubble sheets and short answer responses about my experience. Hey, it was research, and I never became a lifelong swinging bachelor, so I think "no harm, no foul" is in order.

Aside from my admitted family-values detour,

this was a serious duty. I felt like the future of Zenith lay in my choice of plastic for the TV cabinet and the surrounding shape. Were the corners too sharp? What about the hookups on the back? Were they well placed? Did the labeling make sense? Did the auto-search setup feature indeed find all the local over-the-air channels in my area? Success or failure was in my hands.

On a lighter note, when filling out those surveys, I felt like I was one of the team, one of the guys—I thought I could almost go to work with my dad and have a workbench right next to him. I dreamed of someday being old enough where that could be a reality. My dad never took me to a ball game growing up, but this was his ball game.

It's amazing how minutiae that could appear so tedious and trivial held my attention so much. The idea that people like my dad were interested in what I thought about every tiny aspect of their TVs fascinated me. The love of not just paying attention but celebrating, even making a career out of details around some extremely specific thing—I know where I get that from. If anyone ever says I'm "anal retentive," I say "thanks!"

FONTS

*And the lettering is something
called Silian Rail*[17]

—Patrick Bateman, *American Psycho*

1989

My dad had many interests, but there is one outlier I could not explain when I was growing up.

Fonts.

I had no context or theory behind this one. Dad wasn't much of a writer or graphic designer or marketing expert. He never worked in a bookstore or painted signs or banners. Maybe he met some sort of magical Willy Wonka–like typewriter repairman in 1951 with a magic box of movable lead type sets (I have no idea), but when we got our Apple IIGS

---

17 This is the film scene I modeled from scratch that started this book.

and later a 386 DX PC when I was eleven, my dad started on a quest printing out libraries of fonts that went on for years.

And I do mean libraries. In the family computer room, which was already packed full of books and papers, pages of font samples turned into three-ring binders of pages. A few binders turned into half a shelf of binders, all filled with fonts of different sizes, styles, and use cases. I'd come into the den wanting to play a video game, and my dad was already busy with the computer—"I'm printing out fonts!" he'd protest.

One thing Dad wanted and discussed with me in slightly exhausting detail was finding more hollow fonts. This was probably to save ink and allow for cutouts when printing large stencils for painting. There weren't many stencil fonts back then, so when he found a good one he could use and cut with a razor knife and use as a spray-paint template, that was a winner. I am sure by now you think I am exaggerating, but I can still remember my twelve-year-old self occasionally thinking, *Jeez, I wish my dad would stop talking about finding more hollow fonts.*

Maybe the real reason for font madness was that my dad, like me, had the hand-eye coordination you would expect from someone with glasses thicker than

Coke bottles, and he couldn't write by hand to save his life. So being able to label things like wood beams, sheet metal, bicycle parts, just about anything, was something he was always interested in.

Before I wanted to be an engineer, I wanted to be a cartoonist and a writer. Unfortunately, I could barely write or draw by hand. I got a D in handwriting in second or third grade, and it was well deserved—with the psychotic chicken scratches I put down on paper every day at school, I probably should have gotten an F. So I was attracted to the computer. With the computer, my cursed hands didn't matter, and I could finally write stories and draw comics that were legible enough for people to read.[18] I found the computer so freeing that ultimately the act of using the computer to draw and write was almost more important than the drawing or writing itself, so that's how my interests changed.

Years later my dad's font obsession calmed down, yet it had left a permanent impression on me. In my high school journalism class, we would spend a day critiquing the last school newspaper issue, talking

18 My first and only comic strip, at age ten, made on the Apple II GS, was *Tri and Quad*, a comic and straight-man duo of two anthropomorphic shapes that taught kids about geometry, all while Tri made one-liner jokes at Quad's expense. Poor Quad! He always looked so depressed being verbally abused by Tri. I made about ten strips teaching a nonexistent kid readership concepts like area, perimeter, pie charts, and percentages.

about things like story focus and writing style. I was the one who would say, "The caption on page two is in Times, when it should be in Palatino" (which are almost identical—google it). Here's where I should have known I was a little different. I am surprised my journalism teacher did not pull me aside and suggest maybe I was in the wrong class.

One font-related side adventure I had with my dad was calculating headline widths for my journalism class. Back in the nineties, there was still a lot of manual calculation involved in page layout, and one thing we had to do in the class was look at the letters in a headline and count the characters and assign them count values. For example, a small "i," which was rather narrow, was worth 0.5; a capital "M," much wider, was worth 1.5. We would sum up these character counts to get a total number, and this would be a guideline for how many columns a headline would span at different font sizes. I found this to be the most tedious waste of time imaginable. My dad agreed, and together we created a BASIC program to calculate headline widths. It wasn't a huge hit, as it only ran on DOS and all the newspaper work was done on the Mac, but it was still an achievement. Looking back, I feel a little embarrassed, since some of my more programming-savvy peers probably could have written something like this on their own without their dad's help. Still, I was fourteen, it was 1992, and I thought I would be a writer back then, so I've learned to live with it.

Despite my main claims to fame in journalism class being good at counting headlines, cropping photos, and troubleshooting the computers, I kept on with it and ended up graduating with more English credits than anyone else in my high school. Even though I ultimately went into engineering, I inherited my dad's love of printing and typefaces, and ultimately computers, because I was just reaching for a tool to help follow my own dreams.

Whatever our limitations are, what we reach for to overcome them can be as significant as whatever we are trying to overcome and may turn out to be a characteristic that shapes us—so those chicken scratches my dad and I called *handwriting* weren't so bad after all.

WORD SEARCHES

It is not enough to be busy. So are the ants. The question is: What are we busy about?

—Henry David Thoreau

1991

My dad always wanted me to do well in school, mainly in math, and while I wouldn't say he was harsh, he talked to me about school in a way that was a little intimidating—like he knew that there was something large at stake, but he wasn't quite ready to tell me exactly what and why (especially when I was younger). It's not so much that he was a man of few words—it was more that his ability and attempts to explain math, science, and problem-solving gave a few hints of a difficult past. He never went the stereotypical route of complaining about "participation trophies," but there was often a subtle, ominous undertone to how he reflected on learning, studying, and achieving.

Dad used words like "consequence," "misleading," "unfortunate," and "limitation" *a lot* when talking about school. When he thought that some concept was not named well, he would say it was "an unfortunate term," meaning that it was almost tragic that what was not named well risked never being properly understood. When someone talked about "giving points for effort," he'd counter with real-world examples of job-interview candidates who couldn't do what he needed them to do on his team—designing circuits and chips. He didn't resent them for not knowing the answers; he was saddened and saw them as a cautionary tale for me and my sister.

One time he was telling me about a potential hire on his team. "I don't know what to tell some of them [the college grads]—there's no way around it. Even if all the technique is correct, if we don't have the right answer, it doesn't work."

This pensive attitude that would come out in his demeanor when dealing with or talking about school led to a memorable adventure.

When I was in junior high, I had a science teacher, Mr. Yearly, who was, to put it nicely, a little off. He waddled about with a carefree grin in his tent-sized polo shirts, talked at length aimlessly about nothing most class periods—loving the sound of his own voice—and basically looked and acted like if Homer Simpson had a few beers and started one of his long pontifications. My confidence was not inspired. My parents were traditional and always stressed respect for adults, even if I disagreed with them, and to try to keep it together even if I was in a tough situation. Therefore, I didn't say too much about Mr. Yearly, even though I was suspicious that he wasn't exactly teacher-of-the-year material.

This changed after that year's parent-teacher open-house night. My mom and dad finally met this science teacher, Mr. Yearly. Upon arriving home, my dad said that he'd talked to Mr. Yearly, noticed some hobby-related magazines he was reading, and asked about his general interests in science. Surprisingly, my dad delivered this summary of the evening with a bit of a scowl, and he then said something I never would have expected. "Don't listen to anything that man says." He also started supervising what I was learning in science class.

Now that he was on the alert, my dad's first discovery was that Mr. Yearly was fond of giving us word searches for homework, usually with vocabulary from the science lesson, so we'd find words like "cell" and "membrane" in a word search printed out from an Apple IIe a few times a week.

This was one of the few times I'd seen my dad offended. He could not believe that finding a few words mentioned in a lecture in a jumble of letters was what passed for quality, learning, and growth-fostering homework from an education professional. He did not want his son wasting his time with something this pointless. Normally he was too busy to be offended by the world around him, but he made a loud, angry exception here.

This went on for weeks. Every time there was a new word search, there was a new indignant rant from Dad about how ridiculous Mr. Yearly and this class were.

Finally Dad had enough and announced his plan to deal with this situation. Together we wrote a small BASIC application to solve word searches. We would enter the list of lesson words at a prompt, followed by the rows of puzzle letters, and the computer would find the starting position of those words in the rows by looking forward, backward, up, and down. There. Problem solved. No more time on word searches.

I hate to admit it, but having to enter the word search letters into the computer and reading the battleship-like answers we got back ("Amoeba—A4") probably took more time than just solving it myself, but something about this teacher's character spitting out half-baked summaries from a teacher's edition of a textbook and assigning word searches for homework drove my dad into a Captain Ahab–like frenzy to capture and kill mindless busywork. After that adventure, I had a little less respect for teachers but a little more for myself. To this day I am always wary of anyone who does not respect their time or mine, and I never forgot the one time in my life I saw my dad that mad about the principle of something.

It was fitting for my dad that this was a rare occasion though. Being someone who is so busy being productive, helping people, and doing positive things with their life that most things don't annoy or offend them too much is an amazing state of enlightenment to live in. Granted, there are injustices that offend me that I'm willing to fight for, but in a world where people make a career out of Instagram posts shouting about how the new all-female *Ghostbusters* movie ruined their childhood or how pineapple and ham pizza is an abomination, saving your energy and being offended only where it counts is a good thing.

TOP GUN

Confucius allegedly said, "Choose a job you love, and you will never have to work a day in your life." [Pause] I have a few questions about that.

—Steve Mycynek

1991

My dad worked early and late for as long as I can remember, especially when I was in junior high and high school. It's lucky he had a short commute, but that meant he was working almost the entire time he was gone each day. He loved his work, but there was a lot of deadline pressure for many years, as the American electronics industry faced enormous competition from the cheaper, trendier foreign companies like Sony, Panasonic, and Samsung. My dad developed some of the first high-definition television technology at Zenith in the eighties and nineties—a long project that most of us didn't see the results of until after the year 2000.

It was usually dark out when Dad got home. Sometimes we'd already started dinner. Dad was tired from working on custom circuits and boards to compress and decompress the high-detail picture we take for granted today into the same radio air space that normal TV occupied.

As a kid, I used to think it wasn't fair that the Federal Communications Commission (FCC) wouldn't give more "room" for the HDTV signal over the air, but I learned that most of the practical radio frequency ranges, or "bands," in America were all taken—special frequency ranges for the military, for police, the fire department, CB radio, AM/FM, television, and scientific uses. Radio space was just like real estate, and there wasn't much left, so my dad had to find a way to squeeze the HDTV broadcasts of all our favorite programs right next to the traditional ones in the older NTSC analog format we'd all seen since the 1940s. I blamed this constraint for taxing my dad each day. He was always a good dad, but I could feel him reining in crossness and fatigue each evening at dinner and homework time. When dad told me to "take out the trash" or "clean up that mess," I could hear that he was running low on good cheer after a long day.

There are two parts to high-definition television (or any television system). There's the display (something that can show high-resolution video [your screen]) and something that can capture and record it (the high-definition video camera). Camera technology lagged at the time, so the first HDTV content had to come from some other source, and the media that could showcase HDTV's high-quality picture was 35mm film.

Top Gun premiered in 1986. I was a little young to see it in theaters, but I saw bits of it on TV here and there growing up. TV pictures back in the eighties and nineties weren't nearly on par with the movie-theater experience—even on the nicer TVs we watched through my dad's job didn't quite do it justice—but I got enough of the experience watching it on VHS to understand the universal appeal and emotional grip of the story. The desire to be the best, the personal anguish when that's not possible, the temptation to take foolish risks when you feel you have something to prove, and of course, dedicating your life to something that drives you and consumes you—these are magical themes that have stayed with me for years.

Recently, I was at home recovering from dental surgery. I underestimated the pain, and frankly, the dentist did as well, as he only prescribed Tylenol for some crazy reason. What I desperately needed, besides painkillers, was a distraction. *Top Gun* was on Netflix, so I put it on while I iced my jaw and figured out what I'd be able to eat for the next few days. Somehow, as the pain in the section of gum grafted into my lower teeth traveled all the way through the rest of my skull, a decades-old memory came loose as I watched TV—I'd seen a more cinematic presentation of *Top Gun* before, but not in the theater.

I only saw my dad's office at Zenith twice. This was in an era before take-your-child-to-work day and work-life balance, and more in the era of security guards who wore ties, so seeing where he worked was a big deal. One evening, when I was thirteen, my dad told me that the folks at Zenith had a special surprise for us—a demonstration of an early prototype of HDTV.

The next Saturday my whole family piled into the car after lunch and headed to Zenith, the big white building with vertical solid stripes of windows in Glenview, Illinois. My dad led us to a large conference room with a few rows of chairs set up. The lights dimmed, and an announcer spoke over an intercom and said we were going to see an example of a Zenith broadcast of high-definition video with digital surround sound—all transmittable over the airwaves.

That's when I saw what the team chose to demonstrate—the first scene from a scan of the 35mm print of *Top Gun*, in which the main theme goes right into "Danger Zone." I could see every minute detail of those fighter jets taking off the runway. It didn't matter that it was mostly shades of gray on the screen—smoke and steel—I couldn't take my eyes off how much more I could see there than on regular television. I could hear jet engines behind me and over my head—like the roar was coming from a CD player on an enormous stereo rather than a TV speaker though. It was captivating—the way that film was meant to be seen—and the greatest bring-your-child-to-work day ever.

I didn't see anything like that demonstration on television again for many years—I didn't even own an HDTV until long after my dad died. I'm sure it was no accident that the Zenith team chose *Top Gun* for their test-source material—I was watching history in the making of something great, something worth risking and sacrificing for. I wonder what the *Top Gun* moment will be for my daughter, if one is meant to be.

DAD-AMP[19]

In Stereo Where Available
—Television from Generation X

1996

When my grandma and grandpa on my mom's side were getting older, my mom thought it would be a good idea to interview them about their lives, their childhood, their careers, things like that, and videotape it for future generations. We saw my grandparents all the time, but their younger years were still a bit of a mystery to me. When I was eight, I asked my grandma if they had covered wagons like they did on *Little House on the Prairie* when she was

---

19 A play on "WinAmp," an MP3 player from the late nineties.

little,[20] so recording their actual life experiences was probably a good idea.

The next Saturday morning, we headed up to Milwaukee to see Grandma and Grandpa and came prepared to make a day out of Q&A. My mom, being the organized one, had an entire script of questions for her parents, asking them about school, their first jobs, their first apartments, how they spent their free time, married life, and what it was like in general in the first half of the twentieth century. At the time the questions my mom prepared seemed a lot like history class, which was my worst subject by far, and I wasn't interested in hearing what grocery shopping was like in 1940. Still, I was in the AV club in high school (big surprise), so of course I got to proudly serve as director, chief camera operator, and editor. We recorded about four hours of footage. Everything about home video back then was so much more tedious and dorkier than it is today. I had a tripod the size of a parking meter and an extension cord for power, and I even moved the lamps around to get better lighting. We were far away from anyone who would mock me for this setup, though, so I was happy to have an activity for the day.

---

20 My grandma was born in 1913, so no, she did not grow up traveling in covered wagons. She laughed harder than any time I recall when I asked her that and kindly explained that motor vehicles had indeed existed in her youth.

It's too bad we didn't get a video camera until the nineties, as by then my grandma was frail and couldn't speak well. Home video cameras weren't great back then, sound-wise or picture-wise, even with all my careful preparation. When we got home on Sunday, we played back the tape we'd made, and we could barely hear my grandma's voice—after we'd spent hours talking to her and my grandpa on camera! Keep in mind, this was 1996. There was no iMovie or Audacity to clean everything up with a few clicks of something you could download for free, and even with all the free stuff we got from Zenith, we didn't have everything.

Fortunately, this was not a setback.

My dad took me to one of his favorite retailers from the eighties and nineties—Radio Shack. Back then Radio Shack was a real store with real inventory and not just a source of business and investment jokes, so it was always a familiar, happy place. The fact that it was right next to our favorite breakfast-all-day place didn't hurt.

At Radio Shack, we picked up a handful of components. "I have the transistors at home. I need some resistors and capacitors," Dad said. This was long before the Raspberry Pi or BeagleBoard or other electronics kits. Everything was labeled, but there were no kits, no step-by-step guides of what to buy, just part numbers and specs in tiny print on plastic bags the size of postage stamps. My dad knew what to get though, so we were not there long.

With our purchase in hand, we returned home and then went downstairs to the workshop. Now it was time for solder and hot glue.

My dad soldered these few insect-sized components onto a fiberglass board the size of a credit card—he already had a stack of those ready at home. The parts went through the holes in the board, so he then had to flip it over and run wires connecting them, soldering those as well. Finally he hot-glued a plastic mount for a nine-volt battery and four RCA-style stereo connectors—the kind you see on the back of an older DVD player.[21] The entire device was a simple but effective amplifier. We hooked up the video camera to our VHS VCR with the yellow RCA cable for video, but the red and white stereo audio cables passed through this device before reaching the VHS inputs.

After we transferred the Hi8 video recording to VHS, my grandma was ten times louder with no background hum or distortion. Thinking of the squealing of my walky-talkies and cassette recorders cranked up

---

21 RCA was Zenith's main American competitor and has a few everyday electronic standards with their name attached. My sister and I always booed when we saw RCA products—our version of sports rivalry.

to eleven, I exclaimed to my dad, "The sound is so clear—there is no buzz in the background!"

"Of course," he replied. "I used low-noise transistors and low-tolerance resistors."

There was a bit of deadpan here—he honestly didn't understand that I was amazed by what he had done. Because my dad designed television systems and even had a patent on stereo for television (remember those "In Stereo Where Available" banners that popped up on eighties TV shows?), something like this was kids' stuff for him, but he was so low key about it, as if it were no different than someone changing a tire. If this was like changing a tire for him, I could only imagine the real challenges he faced every day at work, like those in the *Top Gun* demo.

What a way to be—to own that level of achievement. To be able to create *ex nihilio*, out of nothing, at a moment's notice, whether the creation is words, pictures, machines, or anything. It's what I want for myself and my children.

THE NO-SHAKING
SECTION

God writes a lot of comedy. . . . The trouble is, he's stuck with so many bad actors who don't know how to play funny.

—Garrison Keillor

1990

I grew up in the Missouri Synod Lutheran church. It always takes me a minute to properly describe the overall feel of that specific Lutheran denomination. It's formal and conservative but not really strict—there are no nuns slapping you with rulers or horror stories about how you're going to hell if you smoke a cigarette. We're more just boring and uptight in oddly specific ways. It's not bad, and

I'll take the Lutherans over some of the other crazies I've met over the decades, but the culture can wear you down.

As German American Lutherans, our secret weapon is that we will bore you to death—possibly with a discussion about how CorningWare is slightly better for reheating casserole but Pyrex is almost as good and it stacks and cleans easier, so it doesn't matter. We love coffee from large five-gallon steel urns in tiny four-ounce Styrofoam cups, which would be infuriating except the coffee is pure acid, so it's actually an appropriate size. There are also a lot of creative Jell-O dishes, and when I say "creative," that's a euphemism for "carrots are involved." We love our church pre-service music, which is exactly what it sounds like. It is the religious equivalent of going to the movies to see the on-screen commercials they show *before* the previews start. When I was six or seven, starting with the pre-service music and all the way through the sermon, I would squirm and complain, and by the first Old Testament reading, my mom would usually give me a pocket calculator to keep me quiet. I'd mash simple arithmetic into it, but it was a scientific calculator—a trade-show giveaway my dad got somewhere—so whenever the pastor would talk about sin, I'd bash the SIN key and watch with glee as the numbers shattered into rows of unpredictable decimal places. Yes, being Lutheran is boring, with little relief, especially as a child.

Over the years, my dad became an usher at our church, which meant getting to the service even earlier. It also meant that he helped with communion and collecting offerings, so when he was on duty, we all sat up front during the service, in a special section for the staff. If only the adventure ended with that.

In the early nineties, when I was twelve, there was a popular movement among many churches to take a brief break from the service about twenty minutes in and shake hands and greet your neighbor and maybe say "peace be with you." It was a little dorky and touchy-feely and felt like something cribbed out of *The Seven Habits of Highly Effective People*, and I have no idea why our church went along with this trend, but I was pummeled by angry preadolescents screaming the MF word at me at junior high during the week (my parents had moved me to a public school by then), so this new attraction barely fazed me.

Getting back to boring and uptight, this "peace be with you" practice did not go over so well with some other older members of the church, though. They resisted. They protested. They did not like this practice of shaking hands and greeting one's neighbor one bit.

If you were foolish enough to try to shake hands with one of these old people during "peace be with you" time, they would literally hold up their hand with the "talk to the hand" gesture and stop you with "Nothing against you, but I'm dead against this."

I wish I were kidding. The one upside was seeing someone with a hearing aid the size of a John Grisham novel say "Talk to the hand."

After a few months of the shakedown trial period, these non-shakers gradually migrated to a small square section in the pews where they could be alone, and no one would try to touch them. What was especially funny was when this divided family members. There was one seventy-five-year-old man named Art, and he was a shaker, but his wife firmly was not. I weep for whatever date night was like for this couple.[22]

The insanity continued as the no-shaking section overlapped with the section where the ushers' families would sit. One Sunday we were all sitting in the shaking demilitarized zone, or whatever you call it, and my dad had to go help with communion set-up before "peace be with you" time.[23] As he stood, he told me gently but firmly, "When the pastor an-

_____

22 Talk to the hand.
23 Also known as "Checkpoint Shakey" and "Don't shake, don't tell."

nounces the greeting time, just sit there and don't do anything."

Of course, I listened, and when the pastor made the announcement for everyone to shake hands, I just sat there frozen. People in the row behind me got up. No one in our row did. Suddenly I saw Art towering over me. He smiled, and I gave him a look that was half afraid, half preteen frustration. He continued to smile down on me and gave me a funny but still friendly look. Then out of nowhere, he patted me on the head like a dog! I think he, too, knew he was trapped in a room full of socially stunted weirdos and was forced to wait it out. I doubt even his seventy-five years of wisdom had prepared him to do or think much more than that, so he improvised.

There's an old expression: "God, please save me from your followers." When people around you are, for lack of a better term, freaking nuts, like my dad said, it's okay to take a break from all of them and let them sort themselves out. You'll still be here if they snap out of it.

THE LAST MOVIE

You left just as you were
becoming interesting.
—Dr. Henry Jones, *Indiana Jones and the*
Last Crusade

1989

A side from all the math homework, model gluing, and circuit building I did with my dad over the years, we still had some non-engineering-related good times. Because television was such big part of the family's legacy, my dad and I consumed our fair share of popular media. Like most kids my age, my dad was there to show me classics like *Star Wars*, *Star Trek*, *The Karate Kid*, and *The Terminator* (that one heavily edited for television). *Deliverance* was on TV once, and that one he had to turn off midway.

The last movie my dad ever took me to see at a theater was *Indiana Jones and the Last Crusade*. I was eleven. If you don't know the movie, it gives some of the backstory of Indiana Jones, famous archaeology professor and jungle explorer, and how he came to be the iconic figure we know and love. The movie introduces Indiana's father, Dr. Henry Jones, a professor too, and a rather difficult, distant man who never fully embraced having a son, at least so it seemed.

This is a perfect time to mention that I was Indiana Jones for Halloween a year or two before that. There's just one small caveat. I didn't dress up in his adventure outfit with the leather jacket and the fedora and the whip. I dressed up in the tweed jacket with the bow tie and glasses he wore when he was teaching at the university! I suspect my dad would have tried to stop me to prevent the inevitable ridicule from the kids at school, but this is also probably about the time he realized he had a little carbon copy of himself running around, so maybe it was too hard to intervene.

"Carbon copy" was not a stretch. Once, my mom was talking to one of her nurse coworkers at her school when I was along to help pack boxes of Band-Aids in the nurse's office. My dad was off in the distance. My mom's friend asked what I was interested in in school, and I started going on about vector-based drawing and how it was different from pixel-based drawing. She smiled at my mom and made this perfect pantomime of someone making a xerox copy of a paper while looking in my dad's direction.

It was and still is great being just like Dad.

But as I'm sure you know, when we meet someone just like us, all the things we don't like about ourselves that we see in them become especially aggravating.

Just like me, my dad wasn't always easy to get along with. He was a flawed human being, just like me, and I'm sure it was as much my fault as his. After the third Indiana Jones movie came out, I entered those awkward years when kids don't get along with their parents. Like I said, Indiana Jones was the last movie.[24] As the years went by, there were fewer father-son activities, but there were plenty of times when my dad and I argued, could never agree or get through a meal without yelling—it was hard.

All those scenes between Indiana and his dad—two bookish, maybe a bit stubborn and grouchy men who were surprisingly resourceful and scrappy when they had to be but still couldn't relate—mirrored our relationship so well when I was in my teens and even

---

24 There were still good times after that, and we did see a small part of *Top Gun* together in his office, as I mentioned in an earlier story.

early twenties. When Indiana's father demands he count to ten in Greek to calm down before speaking, it felt a lot like my dad scolding me—"Don't get your dander up"—when I'd be upset about being a few points off on a junior high math test problem.[25] One time in my teens, I bought some new model rocket gear that was expensive and would launch crafts too high into the air for anywhere in Illinois. He demanded I return it to the store. When I claimed he didn't respect me, he said, "Do I ask 'Where are you going?' 'What are you doing?' 'When will you be back?' No, I expect you'll do things responsibly like we discussed!" His tone was painfully similar Indiana's father reprimanding him. "Did I ever tell you to eat up, go to bed, wash your ears, or do your homework? No. I respected your privacy, and I taught you self-reliance."

With all my dad's pain from his youth, growing up with little family, his fear of poverty and underemployment, his firsthand knowledge of how cold life could be—"cold as sin"—he didn't have the heart, or maybe the emotional vocabulary, to tell me, a teenager, all the scary details of his concerns. So there was a lot of yelling and misplaced anger when he'd react to something he disagreed with. My dad

---

25 I have never heard anyone else use this phrase—I had to look it up to confirm he didn't just make this up.

had a frightening intensity when he tried to get the message out that life wasn't fair. What I know now is that when he was telling me "life isn't fair," it was not to scorn but to warn.

It wasn't until I was a few years out of college that we both calmed down and were able to talk again, much like near the end of the film when Indiana's father finally stops calling him "junior." Once my dad saw that I was living in an inexpensive apartment, wearing inexpensive shirts, and saving the majority of my paycheck each month, we could talk about the future of television, the woodlands, and the workshop, just like when I was a kid. Thankfully, that happened in time, as he died suddenly when I was twenty-six.

Except for the funeral and visitation with the small army of people who came to see us, the week my dad died was a blur. It was like having a high fever for a few days. I went through all the usual grief stages, feeling like I was a bad son, like I didn't listen enough or didn't appreciate him enough, or if I appreciated him more now it would bring him back. The end scenes in *The Last Crusade* where Indiana's father is fatally shot played over and over in my head. The worst part was when it started getting dark out at dinnertime—if I was at the kitchen table,

I'd keep thinking he'd be home from work soon, but he wouldn't be. Thankfully, this is the sort of thing in life that you don't fully get over but you do get through.

I didn't get enough time with my dad, but looking back on these stories, I think he used his time well.

CAUSE AND EFFECT

Though hard to believe, when asked to describe my dad, I'm still often at a loss. Was he an optimist? A pessimist? Kind? Cross? Understanding? Stern? Critical? Curious? Dismissive? Resourceful? Reliable? Generous? Resentful? Silent? Silly? Precise? Obsessive? Prepared?

Yes, he was.

In his sixty-one years, he did so much of so many things for so many that anyone could easily develop any of those impressions of him. Given that even his barber showed up at his funeral, I'm still confident most people saw the positive overall picture. It's not a stretch to say he was a slightly eccentric suburban polymath with a big heart, some sort of MacGyver,

Dr. House, Adam West Batman, Christian Bale Batman, Dr. Henry Jones, Gil Grissom, Leonardo da Vinci type mixed with the Clark Kent from the 1983 *Superman III*. I miss him immeasurably.

I miss my mom too, of course, and she was just as big an influence on me, but her story is so amazing in different ways that I haven't even figured out how to tell it yet.

I hesitate to use my dad's memory to springboard into some self-serving pat on the back, but his legacy lives on through me. All the experiences I had with my dad drove me to create, obsess, create more, and achieve, but to also give, all in the most hands-on way possible. It's hard sometimes. When I work on something, I often feel habits and experiences from decades ago driving me whether I want them to or not.

I shovel and snowplow my neighbors' driveways if they can't do it. If I see one of them has an injury or other issue, I don't even ask—I just try to get it done before anyone notices.

My dad was offended by things that were completely useless. I once saw a manual process at my job that was costing the company tens of thousands to hundreds of thousands of dollars per year, and this bothered me enough that I automated it, and I earned enough bonus money to pay for my daughter's future college education.

If my daughter is doing something in school and I can think of some sort of wood or paper craft that can complement it, I don't just make it—I make it into a kit I can distribute to other parents so they can build it with their own children.

If I'm the third wheel at some volunteer event, that's the perfect time to slip away, find a Dunkin Donuts, and bring back a cardboard box of joe for everyone.

My dad was always prepared. Over twenty years ago, he gave me a set of wide-boring drill bits for no particular reason. As you would guess, he'd often give me lots random things he thought were useful, no matter how unexciting or un-gift-like they appeared. I had little use for them at the time, as I didn't drill a lot of holes over an inch wide, but they've stayed in my toolbox. Recently, I was helping at my daughter's school, setting up some potted plants, and we needed to drill a hole in the bottom of a planter so it could drain. I ran home and got my drill, saw the wide drill bits, and took them. When I got back to the school and took out a drill bit, I realized I was taking the plastic wrap off it for the first time. Even twenty years later, my dad's foresight into being prepared helps me.

The list goes on and on. Why did I build not just a chess puzzle online game but an entire chess set from scratch? Why did I build an interactive children's ABC website? Why did I build a magnetic compass as a graduation gift? I told you—I can't help myself, but as you can now see, it's more than that. For me, embracing just being myself has given me immense power, as I think it can for anyone.

And what about you? Did you think about how you are different in your own way? About your stories? Maybe what you thought of in your life was inspiring, maybe not—maybe it was also painful, boring, silly, or just plain odd. That sounds a lot like my life. Whatever forged you, no matter the peaks, pitfalls, or tragedies, moving with the grain of your inherent state of being will take you far.

I told you my dad used his time well. Because of him, so do I. So can you.

My dad at his desk at Zenith, around 1984